Caring
People

Other titles by Warren W. Wiersbe

Be Myself
The Bible Exposition Commentary: New Testament (2 vols.)
The Bumps Are What You Climb On
The Cross of Jesus: What His Words from Calvary Mean for Us
Elements of Preaching
God Isn't in a Hurry: Learning to Slow Down and Live
The Intercessory Prayer of Jesus: Priorities for Dynamic
  Christian Living
Living with the Giants: The Lives of Great Men of the Faith
The Names of Jesus
On Being a Servant of God
Prayer, Praise, and Promises: A Daily Walk through the Psalms
Run with the Winners
So That's What a Christian Is! 12 pictures of the Dynamic
  Christian Life
The Stategy of Satan
Turning Mountains into Molehills and Other Devotional Talks
Victorious Christians You Should Know
Wiersbe's Expository Outlines on the New Testament
Wiersbe's Expository Outlines on the Old Testament

For Brandon
W.W. Wiersbe
Ps. 16:11

Living Lessons
FROM GOD'S WORD

Caring People

Learning to Live with and Help One Another

Warren W. Wiersbe

Baker Books

A Division of Baker Book House Co
Grand Rapids, Michigan 49516

Published by Baker Books
a division of Baker Book House Company
P.O. Box 6287, Grand Rapids, MI 49516-6287

Previously published under the title How to Be a Caring Christian © 1981 by The Good News Broadcasting Association , Inc.

Second printing, March 2002

Printed in the United States of America

Library of Congress Cataloging-in-Publication Data

Wiersbe, Warren W.
    Caring people: learning to live with and help one another / Warren Wiersbe.
        p.   cm.
        ISBN 0-8010-6387-6
        1. Interpersonal relations–Religious aspects–Christianity. I. Title.
BV4597. W54   20001
241'.677–dc21   2001037872

For current information about all releases from Baker Book House, visit our web site:
                    http://www.bakerbooks.com

Contents

1. We Are Not Alone   7
2. Love One Another   15
3. Wash One Another's Feet   21
4. Pray for One Another   27
5. Edify One Another   37
6. Do Not Judge One Another   45
7. Bear One Another's Burdens   53
8. Serve One Another   59
9. Forgive One Another   67
10. Submit to One Another   75
11. Prefer One Another   83
12. Show Hospitality to One Another   91
13. Do Not Lie to One Another   97
14. Encourage One Another   103
15. Stop Doing That!   113

1
We Are Not Alone

"I believe in individualism," said Franklin D. Roosevelt in his 1936 presidential nomination acceptance speech, "up to the point where the individual starts to operate at the expense of society." Substitute the word "church" for "society," and you have the theme of this book.

God made each of us individuals, and He wants us to cultivate our uniqueness and use it in the special ways He's ordained for us. Peter and Paul preached the same gospel and served the same Lord, but they were unique individuals, not duplicates or copies of somebody else. God has made us a part of His church, and that means we have the responsibility of using our uniqueness to serve Him and His people. We are not alone in our Christian walk. We must have others in our minds and hearts as we pray, study the Word, and serve our Lord.

To understand better this concept of individuality and unity, let's consider some of the images of the church in the New Testament.

We Are Children in the Same Family

"How great is the love the Father has lavished on us, that we should be called children of God. And that is what we are!" (1 John 3:1). We became the children of God through the miracle of the new birth, for "Everyone who believes that Jesus is the Christ is born of God" (1 John 5:1). What a wonder that God should call us to be His own children! Just think, we share His divine nature, enjoy His love and kindness, and one day will share His heavenly home!

But God's family is a large one, and it encompasses the world and spans the generations. During our years of ministry, my wife and I have been privileged to worship and serve with believers in many different countries and cultures, and we have always felt right at home. Denominational or national differences didn't build any walls because we all belonged to the one Father "who is over all and through all and in all" (Eph. 4:6). Age, race, economics, or lack of abilities might prevent me and my wife from joining some of the organizations in our community, but none of those distinctions make any difference when it comes to the church—or they shouldn't. We can sing, "I'm so glad I'm a part of the family of God" and really mean it!

Even though our Father in heaven is perfect, His spiritual family on earth is not. Some of the most miserable people I've met are those who are constantly searching for the perfect church, which usually means, "They do things the way *we* want them done." It's been my privilege to minister to hundreds of congregations in many parts of the nation and the world, and I've learned that God's people are pretty much the same the world over. Every family has its achievers who make us feel proud and its "black sheep" who make us ashamed, but family is family and we have to learn to accept and love one another.

My wife and I were invited to have dinner with a family whose five children ranged in age from a nine-month-old baby to a young teenager. I prepared myself for noise, disorder, and frequent parental warnings, but I was happily disappointed. Never have I seen children display such loving care for each other! A friend who knows the family well assured us that the children's conduct wasn't because there were guests at the table. The children behaved that way all the time. Blessed is that family whose children learn to care for each other!

That's the theme of this book: God's children learning how to care for one another.

We Are Members of the Same Body

After listing some of the trials and burdens he had experienced in his ministry, Paul ended the list with, "Besides everything else, I face daily the pressure of my concern for all the churches" (2 Cor. 11:28). Read his epistles and you will get some idea of why he was pressured with concern. The Philippian church was divided because two women weren't getting along. False teachings had crept into the Colossian church, and legalism was taking over in the Galatian churches. But the congregation that perhaps gave Paul the most trouble was the one for whom he had done the most—the church in Corinth. If you visited the church you would find drunkenness at church suppers, competition and confusion in the worship services, members suing one another, and blatant sexual immorality. Talk about ministry pressure!

When he wrote to the Corinthian Christians to help them solve their church problems, Paul mentioned several images of the church, but the one he emphasized most was that of the body (1 Cor. 12–14). Paul may have used this image because each of us has a body and knows something about how it functions, and because the human body is the ideal picture of unity and diversity. When we trusted Christ, the

Holy Spirit baptized us into His Body and gave us the gift or gifts we would need to minister to the other members of that Body (1 Cor. 12:12–13). In short, as members of the Body of Christ, we belong to each other and we need each other because we minister to each other.

One day my copier wouldn't work. The window of the control panel flashed a number, and I immediately opened the user guide to see what the number was supposed to tell me. I searched in vain for the meaning of that code number. Finally, I phoned the emergency number that the company gave me when I bought the maintenance insurance, and a gracious lady told me that a service agent would be at the house within an hour. He came and quickly repaired the machine and I was back to work. (Now I know what the code number stood for.)

But the human body doesn't function like that because the human body is a remarkable *living* machine totally unlike my copier. When something goes wrong with one part of my body, the other parts temporarily compensate for it until I can get help. If my gall bladder isn't functioning properly, other parts step in until I can get it repaired or taken out. I don't need a flashing light to tell me something's wrong, because my body sends me warning signals—pain—to tell me I need help.

Paul applied this principle to the church. Each member of the Body of Christ has a function to perform so that the Body will grow and remain healthy. Each part is needed, and no part should think it's more important than any other part. (That was the problem in the Corinthian church.) In this way, we minister to one another in the church and together we serve the Lord in this world. A spiritually healthy church is one in which the various "members" know their gifts and use them in the service of Christ and His Body.

In other words, there are no "individualists" who think they can go it alone.

We Are Soldiers in the Same Army

Some people don't like the military images found in the Bible (2 Tim. 2:1–4; Eph. 6:10–18; Heb. 4:12), but that's probably because they misunderstand them. The church is an army to fight Satan and sin, not to fight each other or what Paul called "flesh and blood." "For our struggle is not against flesh and blood, but against the rulers, against the authorities, against the powers of this dark world and against the spiritual forces of evil in the heavenly realms" (Eph. 6:12). There are certainly evil people in this world who oppose Christ and the church, but the evil forces of Satan that use these people are the real enemy. "The weapons we fight with are not the weapons of the world" (2 Cor. 10:4). We depend on prayer and the Word of God (Acts 6:4) as well as the power of the Holy Spirit, for spiritual enemies can be defeated only by spiritual means.

No matter what their rank or responsibility, everybody in the army is important and is expected to do his or her job. Those in command don't give suggestions to be voted on; they give orders to be obeyed. If all the soldiers are in place and obeying orders, there's a better chance to defeat the enemy than if everybody's doing their own thing. Victory depends on strategy, diversity, flexibility, and energy. Each local church needs a God-given strategy for "taking" a city, plus a diversity of people who can do different things. The energy is provided by prayer and the Holy Spirit (Acts 1:8; 4:23–31). But there must also be flexibility so that the strategy can be modified when the situation changes. While spiritual principles never change, ministry strategies do—and "business as usual" isn't likely to win a battle.

Dedicated soldiers keep their eyes open and are alert to do whatever is necessary to help their comrades, even to the point of risking their lives to save others. Good military strategy depends on teamwork. In spite of what people see in war movies, there's not much place for the one-man army in real

11

conflict. It's "one for all and all for one" or there won't be a victory.

We Are Athletes on the Same Team

In New Testament times, athletic games were very important to both the Romans and the Greeks, although the Romans staged them for the entertainment of the spectators, while the Greeks emphasized the physical and moral enrichment of the participants. To the Olympic contestants, the three most important factors were: (1) obeying all the rules in qualifying; (2) obeying the rules while participating; and (3) bringing honor, not just to yourself, but to your land and your city. Even the athletes who participated in solo contests were not acting alone, for they were part of a team and were citizens of a city.

Paul used numerous athletic images in his epistles, including running (Gal. 2:2; Phil. 2:16; 3:12–14), wrestling (Col. 4:12), boxing (1 Cor. 9:25–27), and obeying the rules of competition (2 Tim. 2:5). He also emphasized teamwork, for without team members working together, there can be no victory. Put on the team one "glory hound" who has to make all the points and the team quickly falls apart. Philippians 1:27 and 4:3 use the concept of "teamwork" in the ministry of the local church. The Greek word is *sunathleo,* which means "striving together." (You can see the English word "athlete" in the Greek word.) Philippians 4:3 can be paraphrased "who were teammates with me in the cause of the gospel."

Find a church where God gets the glory and the members don't care who gets the credit, and you'll have a "team" that's making points for the Lord and winning the game. Sad to say, people like Diotrephes, "who love[d] to be first" (3 John 9), still join the team and make it difficult for everybody. What difference does it make who scores the points so long as you win the game? Yes, there are superstars in the world of sports, but not just because of their skill. Superstars are "super" because they know they aren't the only stars in the galaxy and that they'd be falling stars if it weren't for the rest of the team. Imagine trying to play football all alone on the field.

Get the Picture?

There are other images of the church we could look at that also emphasize the fact that we can't live the Christian life in isolation. We belong to each other, we affect each other, and we need each other. The picture is clear: we are either careless Christians or caring Christians.

That's what Paul had in mind when he wrote: "Do nothing out of selfish ambition or vain conceit, but in humility consider others better than [more important than] yourselves. Each of you should look not only to your own interests, but also to the interests of others" (Phil. 2:3–4).

Others . . . in the family . . . in the Body . . . in the army . . . on the team . . . *others*.

Get the picture?

2

Love One Another

One of the biggest misunderstandings in the minds of many Christians is the idea that we can fellowship with God but not be in fellowship with other believers. We can love God and hate God's children! "For anyone who does not love his brother, whom he has seen, cannot love God, whom he has not seen" (1 John 4:20). Of all the "one another" statements in the Bible—and there are more than thirty of them—the one repeated most often is "love one another." The phrase is found at least sixteen times in the New Testament (John 13:34–35 [three times]; 15:12, 17; Rom. 13:8; 1 Thess. 3:12; 4:9; 2 Thess. 1:3; 1 Peter 1:22; 1 John 3:11, 23; 4:7, 11, 12; 2 John 5). "Love one another" is the foundation and the motivation for our obeying the other "one another" statements in the New Testament.

God's Commandment

When our Lord met with His disciples in the upper room before He went to the cross, at least five times He told them to "love one another." This was His "new commandment"

15

for them to obey as His disciples. In fact, their mutual love would be the mark of their discipleship. "All men will know that you are my disciples if you love one another" (John 13:35).

But is it right for God to *command* us to love one another? Isn't love something that really can't be commanded, something that suddenly appears in our hearts and takes command of us? If this is your concept of Christian love, then you've been led astray. Christian love isn't a fuzzy feeling that we manufacture, *it's an act of the will.* Christian love means that I treat others the way the Lord treats me. God listens to me, so I listen to others who want to talk to me. God sacrificed for me, so I sacrifice for others. "God so loved . . . that he gave" (John 3:16). God forgives me, so I forgive others. God's love for us isn't a sentimental feeling that rises and falls with our response. His love is expressed in action, in what He does for the world and for His people.

Christian love is a deliberate act of the will, in which we treat others the way Christ treats us *no matter how they respond.* Even sinners can love those who love them, but believers love those who don't love them—in fact, those who hate them. The more we become like Jesus Christ, the more the world will hate us—and the more we must love as He loved.

In saying that Christian love is an act of the will, I'm not suggesting that there's no emotional content to it at all; but the *willing* comes before the *feeling.* As we act toward others the way Jesus acts toward us, we find our hearts gradually feeling concern for others, and this grows into love. This isn't some psychological trick; it's the work of the Holy Spirit as He makes us more like the Savior. First, we obey the Lord by faith and obey His command to love others. Then, as we keep obeying, we find our obedience becoming more of a "heart experience" as the Spirit works within us. We don't wait for special feelings to take over in our hearts before we love others. We simply obey the Lord, treat other people as He treats us, and trust the Spirit of God to do the rest.

Yes, God has a right to command us to love one another, because Christian love is an act of the will. God's commandments are always God's enablements.

God's Law

"Let no debt remain outstanding, except the continuing debt to love one another, for he who loves his fellow man has fulfilled the law" (Rom. 13:8). The Old Testament Jews had many laws to obey, laws concerning the land, their neighbors and their enemies, religious duties, and even what to eat. But for the Christian believer, every law God ever gave is summed up in "Love one another."

If I love you, I won't lie about you, steal from you, covet what you own, or even think about taking your life. The moral law of God still stands and a righteous God still demands righteous living, but the motivation for that righteousness is love and not law. It's not fear of punishment but love of God that moves us to obey. It's not compulsion from the outside but compassion on the inside that encourages us to obey God's will.

Love isn't a substitute for the law, but love enables us to obey the law. I doubt that most Christian believers ever think about laws and punishments. Their motivation is much higher: they love because God first loved them.

God's Teaching

First Thessalonians 4:9 tells us that we "have been taught by God to love each other." God is love and He wants His children to be filled with love.

God the Father has taught us to love each other by giving His beloved Son to be the Savior of the world. God the Son has taught us to love one another, not only by His words, but also by the example of His life on earth and His suffering and death on the cross. "Greater love has no one than this, that one lay down his life for his friends" (John 15:13). But Jesus went even further. He laid down His life for His *enemies!* The Holy Spirit teaches us to love each other by filling our inner person with divine love. "God has poured out his love into our hearts by the Holy Spirit, whom he has given us" (Rom. 5:5).

It's one thing to learn the lesson and quite something else to practice it. The more we meditate on God's love for us in sending His Son, and the more we consider Christ's love in dying for us on the cross, the more the Holy Spirit will fill our hearts with the love of God. This is one reason why Jesus gave His church the Lord's Supper, so that we will remember that He gave His body and shed His blood for us.

God's Nature

Christian love is one of the "birthmarks" of God's children. "Everyone who loves has been born of God and knows God" (1 John 4:7). God is love (1 John 4:8, 16), and if we have God's nature within, we will want to love. Love for others is the normal response of the born-again believer. "Love one another deeply from the heart," wrote Peter, "for you have been born again" (1 Peter 1:22–23).

The old nature (what Paul called "the old man" or "the flesh") is not very loving, and it loves the things that are wrong. Before we trusted Christ, "we too were foolish, disobedient, deceived and enslaved by all kinds of passions and pleasures. We lived in malice and envy, being hated and hating one another. But when the kindness and love of God our Savior appeared, he saved us" (Titus 3:3–5). What made the difference? The kindness and love of God!

Peter cautions us that our love should be "sincere" (1 Peter 1:22) and not just religious pretense. Sincere love is true love, the love of God expressed in all that we do and say. There's an artificial kind of emotion that tries to pass for love, but it's shallow and doesn't last. Peter also tells us that our love must come from the depths of our being. It must not be something that we turn on and off like a radio. So, true Christian love is sincere, it comes from deep within, and it is the natural expression of the new nature within.

God commands us to love. When we trust Christ, God puts His own nature within us by His Holy Spirit so that we can obey His commandment. As we obey Him, we manifest His love before a selfish and loveless world, and people discover that they too can trust Christ and become new creatures. "No one has ever seen God," says 1 John 4:12, "but if we love each other, God lives in us and his love is made complete in us." How do we make the invisible God visible to a watching world? By loving one another and sharing that love with those who have never trusted Christ. During the early days of the church, the pagan Romans and Greeks would look at the Christians and exclaim, "Behold, how they love one another!"

Does the church have that kind of witness today?

Caring Christians are people who love others.

3

Wash One
Another's Feet

Loving one another in Christ is a very practical thing. It's not a matter of words only but also of deeds. It's one thing to say "I love you" to another Christian but quite something else to prove it by our actions. In the upper room, where Jesus met with His disciples before His arrest and crucifixion, He demonstrated His love for them by doing what they wouldn't do: He washed their feet.

> Jesus knew that the Father had put all things under his power, and that he had come from God and was returning to God, so he got up from the meal, took off his outer clothing, and wrapped a towel around his waist. After that, he poured water into a basin and began to wash his disciples' feet, drying them with the towel that was wrapped around him.
>
> John 13:3–5

This was a sermon in action, and we want to consider what Jesus did, what He is doing now, and what He wants us to do.

What Jesus Did

Jesus is Lord and Master, yet He washed His disciples' feet. He is God in human flesh, yet He washed His disciples' feet. Washing feet was the menial task of a servant, so Jesus humbled Himself and became a servant. What He did that evening was a demonstration of Philippians 2:5–11, a passage that describes our Lord's willing descent from heaven to the cross. He humbled Himself and became obedient to death—"even death on a cross."

No miracle can be explained, but especially the miracle of our Lord's incarnation can't be explained. Jesus is eternal God; He existed with the Father and the Spirit before creation, before time began. But He chose to lay aside His glory and His own will to come to earth as a baby, grow up, and then die on a cross. He could have come as a triumphant general or a glorious king, and that would have pleased the Jewish people; but He chose to come as a baby who became a suffering servant.

In John 8, Jesus stooped down to write with His finger in the sand, and the result was the forgiveness of a sinner, the woman taken in adultery. In John 13, Jesus stooped again, this time to wash His disciples' feet. I wonder if John chose these two incidents to teach us that Jesus, in His incarnation, "stooped" to our level so that He might save sinners and cleanse believers.

What Jesus Is Doing Now

Our Lord is now in heaven as our High Priest and our Advocate (Heb. 4:14–16; 1 John 2:1–2). As High Priest, He intercedes for us and gives us the grace we need to obey Him and say no to temptation. We can come to His throne of grace and ask for all that we need for all the trials and temptations that we face. If we do sin, Jesus is our Advocate who "speaks to the Father in our defense" (1 John 2:1). This doesn't mean that the Father wants to punish us and that the Son changes the Father's mind, because the Father and the Son are in perfect agreement on everything. Both the Father and the Son want to cleanse the believer who has sinned, and the death of Jesus on the cross makes this possible. When we confess our sins, He is faithful to His promise and just to His Son who died for our sins, and that enables the Father to forgive His children when they come to Him (1 John 1:9).

This wonderful transaction is pictured in our Lord's washing of the disciples' feet. When sinners receive Christ as Savior, they are washed all over and made clean; but as believers walk in this world, their feet become defiled and must be washed. Jesus knew that His followers wouldn't and couldn't live sinless lives, so He made provision for their daily cleansing. Christians don't need to be saved over and over again when they sin, because a person is born into God's family but once. What we need to do is to confess our sins and ask Jesus to wash our feet so we can stay in fellowship with Him and with one another.

"Unless I wash you," said Jesus, "you have no part with me" (John 13:8). The word "part" carries the meaning of sharing or partnership, which in John 15 Jesus called "abiding" in Him. It has to do with fellowship, not sonship. When believers sin, they don't lose their spiritual sonship, but they break their spiritual fellowship with the Lord, and this renders them powerless to serve the Lord acceptably. Just as the Old Testament priests had to wash their hands and feet in the laver in the sanctuary court, so God's New Testament priests must come to the Savior for His cleansing. When Our Lord washed the disciples' feet, He was illustrating 1 John 1:9 and Psalm 51.

What Jesus Wants Us to Do

Jesus wants us to follow His example. "I have set you an example that you should do as I have done for you" (John

23

13:15). He didn't say that we should do *what* He did but *as* He did. What did He do? He humbled Himself and served others. He took the place of a servant.

The example of humility. Humility is that grace that when you know you have it, you've lost it. All of us have heard about the man who wrote the book *My Great Humility and How I Attained It.* Humility doesn't mean that we think meanly of ourselves, but that we don't think of ourselves at all. Humility is what Jesus illustrated in washing the disciples' feet and what Paul discussed in Philippians 2.

The world asks, "How high are you?" But the important question is "How low are you?" The world wants to know how many people work for us, but Jesus wants to know how many people we serve. Are we washing others' feet as Jesus did?

Keep in mind that before this happened, the disciples had been debating about who among them was the greatest (Luke 22:24–30). When Jesus knelt before them and washed their feet, they must have felt very ashamed of themselves. As the children of God, our job isn't to become famous and important, but to be busy serving others and helping them to be clean. We should be the kind of persons that leave others cleaner than when we found them.

The secret of humility. Humility doesn't come from looking at yourself and seeing how poor you are. It comes from looking to Christ and seeing how rich you are. Jesus knew that the Father had put all things in His hands (John 13:3), so He took a towel in His hands and served His disciples. If you had everything in your hands, would you pick up a towel and become a servant?

The secret of humility comes with the realization that you are God's child through faith in Jesus Christ and that you have all things in Christ (Eph. 1:3; 1 Cor. 3:21–23). God's children don't have to pretend to be wealthy; they are wealthy in Christ! They don't have to act like kings; they are kings—and that's precisely why they can stoop and become servants.

The practice of humility. What does it mean to wash others' feet? It simply means to serve them and leave them better than you found them. It means to refresh Christians who are discouraged and need a new start. Paul wrote about saints who had refreshed his spirit (1 Cor. 16:17–18; Rom. 15:30–33; 2 Cor. 7:14; 2 Tim. 1:16–18; Philem. 7, 20). Some of them met his material needs; some brought good news of answered prayer; some spoke encouraging words to the apostle and gladdened his heart.

Are you a "refreshing saint" who serves others and sends them on their way with new hope and power? Or are you the kind of Christian who waits for everybody else to serve you? Do we help others have cleaner feet, and are we willing to humble ourselves to minister to them? Remember, the blessing doesn't come from knowing about this but by doing it. "Now that you know these things," said Jesus, "you will be blessed if you do them" (John 13:17).

Jesus points the way to humbleness, holiness, and happiness, a life of following His example and stooping to serve others.

Christians who care will wash the feet of others.

4

Pray for One Another

Confess your trespasses to one another, and pray for
one another."

—James 5:16 NKJV

"At least I can pray for you" is a statement God's people
often make, but it's a statement that can be misleading. Prayer
isn't the *least* thing we can do for people—it's the *greatest* thing
we can do! It's no insignificant thing to touch the throne of
God by faith and see the power of God released to meet the
needs of His people. The English spiritual writer William Law
wrote, "He who has learned to pray has learned the greatest
secret of a holy and a happy life." We might expand that
statement and say, "Those believers who have learned to pray
for others have entered deeper into the secret of a holy and
happy life."

James concluded his book by exhorting us to be patient
(5:7–11) and to be prayerful (vv. 12–18), because prayer and
patience go together. It's through faith and patience that we
inherit what God has promised us (Heb. 6:12), and often we
have to wait on the Lord before the answer comes (Pss. 37:7;
40:1). This isn't because God can't do what He wants to do

when He wants to do it, but because too often we're not really prepared to receive the answer. Not only must we be prepared to pray, but we must also be prepared for the answer when it comes. If we aren't prepared, we may rejoice more in the answer than in the Giver and fail to bring glory to His name.

As you read the Epistle of James, you discover that he wrote to a group of believers who were experiencing many different trials, not unlike our churches today. Among other trials, some of the laborers weren't receiving their wages (5:4), other people in the fellowship were sick (5:14), and some were creating divisions in the church (4:1ff.). "Is any one of you in trouble? He should pray" was the solution James gave to their problems (5:13). Too often praying is the last thing we do when it ought to be the first thing.

The Prayer Tie That Binds

God's people are bound together by many sacred ties—the indwelling Holy Spirit and the love He puts in our hearts for each other; our hunger to know the Word of God; our devotion to the Lord in worship; our concern for a lost world. But one of the strongest ties is the joy we find in praying for one another and seeing God answer prayer.

> There is a scene where spirits blend,
> Where friend holds fellowship with friend,
> Though sundered far, by faith they meet,
> Around one common mercy seat.
> Hugh Stowell

In order for me to pray for other believers, I must first know them and be close enough to them to recognize the burdens they carry. That means I must be part of a local church and regularly meet together with the saints for worship, service, and prayer. The Bible knows nothing of isolated Christians, for "we are his people, and the sheep of his pasture" (Ps. 100:3). It's the nature of sheep to flock together. When we pray for one another, we build the unity of the church and contribute to the spiritual maturity of the people as well as our own maturity.

Christian worship involves the horizontal plane as well as the vertical one. We look up and worship our wonderful Lord, but we also look around at His people and show concern for one another. How can I grow in my love for the Lord if my heart is cold toward His people? Our focus of attention in worship is on the Lord, but that worship must increase our love for others or else we are only fooling ourselves.

Praying for one another means more than simply obeying His commandment. It's entering into a gracious privilege given to us by the Lord, a privilege that brings blessings to the whole church, including ourselves. To look at it another way, *not to pray for others is to sin,* as the words of Samuel the prophet make clear: "Moreover, as for me, far be it from me that I should sin against the LORD in ceasing to pray for you" (1 Sam. 12:23 NKJV). Prayer for others opens up so many doors of blessing that it's a wonder we don't make prayer a greater priority in our lives and our churches!

You've noticed, I'm sure, that the "Disciples' Prayer" (or "Lord's Prayer") is a family prayer and that the pronouns are plural. We say "our Father," not "my Father." As we pray for our own needs we also pray for the needs of others. "Give us this day our daily bread . . . forgive us . . . lead us not into temptation." Although we may pray in solitude, we never pray alone, for we're part of a praying family around the world. This should encourage us even more to "pray one for another."

Praying for the Sick (5:13–16)

The sick and physically afflicted usually get the most attention when churches compile their prayer lists, and there's nothing wrong with this. Jesus had compassion on the sick and afflicted and so should we. But it takes spiritual discernment to know how to pray for these suffering people. Are they suffering because God is training them and helping them mature, or is He disciplining them because they've disobeyed His will? Do they have sins to confess? If so, then the spiritual leaders of the church ought to be present (private sins—private confession; public sins—public confession). Are there those in the group who have the gift of faith from the Lord to pray for healing? The miracle actually comes from the interceding and not the anointing. In praying for the sick, we shouldn't simply recite names on a list and ask God to heal them. We don't always know His will in these matters, so we must be sure that the Spirit is guiding us.

The fact that believers are sick or afflicted isn't evidence that the Lord is displeased with them or chastening them because of sin. God allowed Paul to have a thorn in the flesh for the purpose of keeping him humble (2 Cor. 12:1–10). Paul prayed three times that the Lord would remove the pain and distress, but the Lord refused to do so. Paul's prayers didn't bring him healing, but they did bring him the grace he needed to transform his affliction into blessing, for in his weakness and pain he discovered spiritual strength. The transformation of pain is perhaps a greater miracle than the removal of the cause of pain.

Praying for the Wayward (5:16, 19–20)

In almost every church, there are sheep who go astray and need our prayers. When I was serving in pastoral ministry, I kept a list of the names of people whose Christian walk concerned me, and I faithfully prayed for them. I recall a husband whose careless life was breaking his wife's heart, and I prayed daily for him, telling the Lord I would speak to this man when He opened the door. After all, "Faith without works is dead" (2:20). A few days later, I stepped into a restaurant and there he sat! I asked if I could join him, and during that lunch conversation, the Lord met his need and brought him back to the fold. His wife was praying for him and so were his friends, and the Lord graciously answered.

However, the problem is that many believers are embarrassed to share these personal needs with their pastor, let alone the church family. We can understand their concern, because some Christians hear and pray while others hear and gossip. But we shouldn't bear these burdens alone. Every believer needs a confidential prayer partner who will talk to God about the need and not to anybody else. Better yet is a small confidential prayer group.

No matter how wayward that loved one or friend might become, God is still on the throne and will answer in His time. *Never give up on anybody!* When Satan tempts us to quit praying, that might be a signal that God is about to answer—so keep praying!

Praying for God's Servants

I count it a privilege to pray daily by name for our church's ministry staff and for a number of missionaries and Christian leaders. When I served as a pastor, I thanked God for those who prayed for me. When asked the secret of his effective ministry, Charles Spurgeon replied, "My people pray for me." In fact, Paul's requests can guide us in our own praying as we intercede for pastors, teachers, missionaries, evangelists, Christian executives, and all who seek to serve the Lord.

Pray that God will protect them (Rom. 15:31a). Paul was a marked man who constantly needed God's protection. He traveled a great deal and found himself in many different kinds of circumstances (see 2 Cor. 11:23–33). There were religious bigots who would have killed Paul if God hadn't guarded him. I have the itineraries of several of my friends and I pray for them daily, that God will care for them, assist them in travel, watch over their luggage, and take them safely to their destinations. Satan is a murderer (John 8:44) and would kill all of us if he could, especially those of God's servants who are having an impact in this world.

But even local ministers whose names aren't known outside their own circle need the prayers of their people. Every faithful servant of the Lord is a target for the enemy, because there are professed believers everywhere who like to create problems for pastors. Some of these people are just nuisances who are looking for attention, time-wasters who run from church to church with their imaginary problems. But there are also determined enemies of the gospel in every community who hate God and the church and want to see God's work discredited and destroyed. Sometimes they're in places of authority in the local government where their decisions can greatly affect God's work.

Pray that God will bless their ministry (Rom. 15:31b–32). Paul didn't take it for granted that God would automatically bless his ministry just because he was an apostle. When he wrote these words to the Roman Christians, he was on his way to Jerusalem to deliver a special offering from the Gentile churches. He wanted to be a peacemaker and not a troublemaker. Unfortunately, not all the Jewish believers understood and appreciated Paul's ministry to the Gentiles.

Pastors and other ministers of the Lord work hard week after week as they study the Word, pray, minister to people personally, and seek to share Christ, and they need our prayer help. We need to pray for those who plan and direct the public worship of the church, the educational programs, and the evangelistic and missionary outreach. Paul had been to heaven and back and had personally seen and heard Jesus Christ, yet he pleaded with people to pray for him. If he needed prayer support, how much more do we?

Pray that God will open doors for them (Col. 4:2–4). True servants of God don't *pry* doors open; they *pray* them open.

"Knock and the door will be opened to you" (Luke 11:9). Paul was a prisoner in Rome when he wrote this request, but he didn't ask that the saints pray for his release. Rather, he was concerned that God open his mouth and give him the right things to say to the right people in the right way at the right time. God's servants need discernment to see these open doors, and they need faith to be able to walk through them for His glory. A lost opportunity may not be found again. Many a flourishing ministry today began simply as an open door that somebody was discerning enough to see and believing enough to enter, trusting God for what lay ahead.

Pray that each servant will have a good conscience (Heb. 13:18). In recent years, we have witnessed the failures and falls of some high-profile Christian leaders, tragedies that have affected the testimony of the whole church. Paul always sought to have a "conscience without offense toward God and men" (Acts 24:25 NKJV). When the servant of God begins to worry more about reputation than character, the conscience begins to deteriorate. Secret sin leads to a defiled conscience (1 Tim. 1:15), and if that sin isn't confessed and forsaken, it will lead to an evil conscience (Heb. 10:22) that calls good evil and evil good. We must never assume that all Christian workers are walking close to the Lord or that they are never tempted to disobey.

A friend of mine and his wife were visiting garage sales one Saturday and he saw a lovely piece of framed calligraphy of Jude 24—"Now unto him that is able to keep you from falling, and to present you faultless before the presence of his glory with exceeding joy." He said to his wife, "I'm going to buy that for Warren to put in his study." He gave it to me and it hangs today in my study, as a reminder that I can fall just like any other person, but that Jesus can keep me from falling. Best of all, until the Lord called him home to heaven, my friend backed up his gift with his prayers for me.

Praying Bible Prayers

Most of us pray the Bible promises and thank God for them, but what about the Bible prayers? The Spirit of God inspired the prayers recorded in Scripture and we can use them as we pray for ourselves and for others. Ephesians 1:15–23 is a prayer for wisdom and for spiritual insight into the Word of God and the will of God. Ephesians 3:14–21 focuses on spiritual stability and power, and Philippians 1:9–11 is a pastor's loving prayer for his people to grow in spiritual maturity. Colossians 1:9–12 opens to us the fullness of God as found in Jesus Christ. In the psalms we find prayers for every situation of life, as well as the praise we ought to give to the Lord when He answers prayer. In fact, even the doctrinal passages in the Bible can be turned into prayers of thanksgiving and praise as we realize what the Lord has done for us. Often while reading about Christ's words and deeds as recorded in the Gospels, I have lifted my heart in prayer and praise and asked Him to make these blessings realities in my own life.

Praying for the Lost

"Brothers, my heart's desire and prayer to God for the Israelites is that they might be saved" (Rom. 10:1). Paul prayed that prayer while writing one of the most theologically profound sections of the Word of God, chapters that emphasize the sovereignty of God. If theology is divorced from ministry—especially evangelism—it becomes cold and mechanical. In contrast, for Paul, knowing God better was a stimulus to sharing Him more. How can we study the character and works of the glorious Lord and ignore His love for lost sinners? The Bible says that God is "not wanting anyone to perish" (2 Peter 3:9) but "wants all men to be saved" (1 Tim. 2:4). If your theology keeps you from having a sincere burden for the lost, there's something wrong with your theology.

We ought to begin by praying for the lost people in our family and our neighborhood, people we know and to whom we can share a witness for the Lord. As we sincerely intercede for people, we discover that God gives us opportunities to share Christ with them in a very natural way. We also need to pray for the lost in Sunday school classes, children's groups and youth clubs, adult "growth groups," and Bible studies.

In one of the congregations I pastored, God gave us a wonderful single lady who devoted her life to teaching boys and girls in the primary department. Whenever one of her former pupils responded to a public invitation to receive Christ, Mary would come up to me after the service and say, "Pastor, I've been praying for her (or him) for the past seven years." No child she had taught ever escaped the power of her prayers, and today in that church, there are faithful members who came to Christ partly because Mary interceded with the Lord for their souls. Even more, some of her former pupils entered full-time Christian service and went out to win others.

Intercessory prayer is one of the believer's greatest privileges. When we pray for others, we stand with the giants of Bible history—Abraham, Moses, Samuel, David, the prophets and the apostles, and Jesus Himself.

"There is nothing to be valued more highly," wrote Oswald Chambers, "than to have people praying for us; God links up His power in answer to their prayers."

If others are praying for us, shouldn't we be praying for others?

5

Edify One Another

Christians who care will edify one another in the things of the Lord. The word "edify" comes from a Latin word that means "to build up." Our English word "edifice" comes from that same word. Christians who care will seek to build others up in the faith. "Let us therefore make every effort to do what leads to peace and to mutual edification" (Rom. 14:19).

How can I help others grow in Christian life and service? How can others help me grow? Each believer ought to be a part of a local fellowship and in that fellowship minister to others. By ministering to each other, we help each other grow.

There are two kinds of people in this world: those who destroy and those who build. There are those who edify, and there are those who tear down. It takes very little effort and time to destroy something, but it takes wisdom and patience to build. It's much easier to be a destroyer than a builder, but God wants us to be builders. He doesn't want us to go through life tearing down people, churches, Sunday school classes, or families. He wants us to edify others and help to build the church.

Our Example

God has given us a number of spiritual tools to use for building one another up. The first tool is *our own personal example*. The key text is Romans 14, where Paul seeks to answer the problem of Christians disagreeing among themselves. The weak Christians in the Roman assemblies (probably Jewish believers) wouldn't eat all foods, and they criticized the strong Christians (probably Gentiles) who believed that they could. The Jewish believers celebrated their holy days while the Gentile Christians treated each day alike. These differences over days and diets created serious dissension in the church, and this dissension led to division.

"Therefore let us stop passing judgment on one another," Paul wrote in verse 13. "Instead, make up your mind not to put any stumbling block or obstacle in your brother's way." The way we live, worship, and serve the Lord, affects other people and either builds them up or tears them down. "I am fully convinced that no food is unclean in itself. But if anyone regards something as unclean, then for him it is unclean. If your brother is distressed because of what you eat, you are no longer acting in love. Do not by your eating destroy your brother for whom Christ died. Do not allow what you consider good to be spoken of as evil. For the kingdom of God is not a matter of eating and drinking, but of righteousness, peace and joy in the Holy Spirit" (vv. 13–17). In other words, the strong Christians shouldn't use their freedom in Christ to tear down the weak Christians, and the weak Christians shouldn't criticize the strong ones for enjoying their freedom. They should receive one another in Christ because the Lord has received them (14:1; 15:7), and they should help one another grow.

Remember that the strong Christians were those in the church who accepted their freedom in Christ and realized that all foods were clean and should be enjoyed. (See Mark 7:14–23; 1 Tim. 4:1–5; 6:17.) But mature Christians must be very careful not to run ahead of the weaker Christians who still need time to grow. You can't force maturity on somebody else any more than you can force a baby to grow. It takes a great deal of patience, love, and kindness to bring a child to mature behavior.

In Jesus Christ we have freedom, but if we use that freedom selfishly, we may destroy somebody else who isn't ready for the demands of freedom. I can go places that might not hurt me, but my example might hurt somebody else. I might engage in activities that wouldn't destroy me, but my example might destroy someone else. When my wife and I were first married, we were not too worried about leaving knives or scissors on the table, but when our children came along, we were careful to make sure that the knives and scissors were out of their reach. The children had to grow first and learn how to use adult tools. It may not be a sin to leave a safety pin on the floor, but if that pin hurt one of our children who was playing on the floor, then my carelessness was a sin.

The first tool we use for edifying one another is our own example. Is your example as a Christian tearing people down or building them up? Are you flaunting your freedom in Christ or controlling that freedom in love? Our job isn't to argue other believers into agreeing with us; our job is to help other believers get closer to the Lord so they will glorify Him. When we're all abiding in Christ, we'll have an easier time agreeing with each other and manifesting true Christian unity.

Our Speech

The second tool that God gives us to help others grow is *speech*. "Do not let any unwholesome talk come out of your mouths, but only what is helpful for building others up according to their needs, that it may benefit those who listen" (Eph.

39

4:29). As we speak to one another about the Lord and what He's doing in our lives, we help others to grow in grace.

You can't see spoken words, but spoken words have great power. The foreman of a jury says, "We find the defendant guilty," and those five words put a prisoner behind bars. "The tongue has the power of life and death," says Proverbs 18:21. This means that our words and the way we speak them can kill or make alive. Have you ever had someone come to you on a dark, dismal day and speak a word of encouragement that changes your whole outlook? Their gracious words make the sun come out! On the other hand, have you ever been feeling really great when somebody comes along and criticizes you, or perhaps you receive a critical letter, and then the sun disappeared? Words have power to encourage or discourage, to build up or tear down.

According to Ephesians 4:15, we must speak the truth in love. To edify others, we need both truth and love. It has well been said that love without truth is hypocrisy, and truth without love is brutality—and we don't want to be guilty of either sin! When we speak the truth in love, our words minister grace to our hearers. Our speech ought to always be "full of grace, seasoned with salt," we are told in Colossians 4:6. There ought always to be graciousness about our speech that comes from a heart filled with love. We edify one another by our example, and we edify one another by our speech, and the two work together.

Our Spiritual Gifts

God gives us a third tool for edifying the church, and that's the ministry of our *spiritual gifts.* "Since you are eager to have spiritual gifts, try to excel in gifts that build up the church" (1 Cor. 14:12).

The people in the Corinthian church were using their spiritual gifts as weapons to fight with, or toys to play with, rather than as tools to build with. They competed with one another in displaying their gifts, and this was hurting the church. This was a very gifted church; in fact, Paul said that they didn't lack any spiritual gift (1:4–7). But they were using their gifts to show off and not to build up as they competed with one another.

God gives us spiritual gifts, not so we can exhibit them and look important, but so we can build up other believers and strengthen the church. The services conducted in the Corinthians' assembly were doing the people more harm than good. Paul said, "When you meet together it is not for the better but for the worse" (11:17 AMP). It's unfortunate that when God's people get together they create rivalry, bickering, and competition instead of unity and mutual edification. People go home from such meetings in worse shape than when they came! All things should be done "for the strengthening of the church" (14:26).

This means that when the church gathers together, the singing ought to be edifying, the teaching and the preaching of the Word ought to be nourishing. Even fellowshipping at a meal ought to be edifying as the church gathers together. There's certainly nothing wrong with God's people eating together, but the fellowship ought to provide food for the soul as well as for the body.

We should use our spiritual gifts to build up other Christians, and other Christians will help to build us up. Too often we go to church services with the wrong attitude, asking, "Well, what am I going to get out of it?" Then we come home and say, "I didn't get anything out of going to church today!" But we ought to go to the assembly asking, "What can I put into it? How can I help somebody else grow in the Lord?" That word of encouragement, that brief time of fellowship or prayer, could mean so much in the life of another Christian. So the next time you find yourself with God's people in God's house, pray to the Lord, "Help me to use the gifts you've given me to encourage others and help them grow."

Our Love

Love is a fourth tool God has given us for building one another up. First Corinthians 8:1 states, "Knowledge puffs up, but love builds up." All of us know people who are well-educated but fail to use their knowledge constructively. They know the Word of God, but they don't use spiritual truth to edify the church. They use their knowledge to impress people, or perhaps to argue, and too often they go from church to church creating problems. Paul said, in effect, "You have knowledge, and that's fine. But knowledge will puff up and inflate your ego. Love will build up." He wasn't saying that believers have to make a choice between love and knowledge, because God wants us to speak the truth in love (Eph. 4:15) and to use our knowledge in love.

When you share your knowledge of God's Word, do it in love. Whatever you do for God, do it in love, because love builds up. It builds you up and also builds up the people you minister to. This means we must have the love of God in our hearts and obey our Lord's new commandment. "A new command I give you: Love one another" (John 13:34). It's impossible to build people up if we're angry, proud, or authoritarian. We must do everything in love because love builds up.

According to 1 Corinthians 13, Christian love shows itself in many different ways, such as in patience, kindness, gentleness, and sacrifice. Love builds up, and love should be the motivation of all that we do in serving the Lord. When there's an atmosphere of love in the local church, it helps the immature believers grow up faster and the mature believers show more concern for them.

Our Prayers

Colossians 4:12 tells us that we build each other up when we pray for each other. This verse is about Epaphras, who was probably the founder of the church in Colosse. Paul told the Colossians that Epaphras was "always wrestling in prayer" for them that they might "stand firm in the will of God, mature and fully assured." As we pray for people, God is able to work in their lives and build them up. Prayer is one of the most important tools for building up the church.

I hope you don't just pray generally, "Lord, bless the church and bless our family." I hope you have a prayer list. Pray specifically. I suggest you make a list of the people and ministries about which you're concerned, divide the list by seven, and pray for a certain number each day. It's a wonderful thing to pray specifically for people and ministries because God uses specific prayers to build people up in the faith. There might be some concerns you feel burdened to pray for every day, so have a daily prayer list as well. However you do it, spend time daily praying specifically for people and ministries, and God will use your prayers to build His church.

God's Word

In Acts 20:32 Paul said, "Now I commit you to God and to the word of his grace, which can build you up and give you an inheritance among all those who are sanctified." The Word of God is a basic tool for building up God's people. When you discuss people's personal problems with them, use the Word of God to shed light on those problems. When people phone to complain about something, use the Word of God to deal with those complaints. Drop the Word of God into your conversation. Don't go around beating people over the head with the Bible or quoting Scripture all the time, but do use the Word of God discreetly because it builds people up.

If we spend time daily in the Word, we'll grow ourselves and have truth in our hearts that we can use to encourage others. It's a mark of a growing Christian that he or she is led by the Spirit to share just the right verse from Scripture to meet the immediate need. Like a physician who has just the right medicine, the Spirit-led Christian has just the right promise or admonition from the Word to help build others up.

Are you a destroyer or a builder? Is God using you to build up the church and other saints? Anybody can tear things down, but Christians who care build things up. Christians who care edify one another.

6

Do Not Judge
One Another

Caring Christians do not judge one another. "Therefore let us stop passing judgment on one another" (Rom. 14:13). "The man who eats everything must not look down on him who does not, and the man who does not eat everything must not condemn the man who does, for God has accepted him" (v. 3).

A great deal of judging goes on among Christians, doesn't it? I wonder sometimes if judging one another is not the chief "indoor sport" of some of God's people. In Scripture, the Lord has laid down some important guidelines for all of us to help us in this matter of judging.

We Must Have Discernment

To begin with, we must have discernment as we mature in the Christian life. Christian love is not blind. Paul prayed for the Philippians: "And this is my prayer: that your love may abound more and more in knowledge and depth of insight, so that you may be able to discern what is best and may be pure and blameless until the day of Christ" (Phil. 1:9–10). His prayer was that they might have loving discernment and careful discernment. Without discernment, we can't possibly make wise decisions about our own character and conduct, let alone the character and conduct of others.

Some people tell us that God's love is so great that we should just love everybody regardless of how they behave. Certainly we should love other believers and love lost souls. We're even commanded to love our enemies. But in exercising Christian love, we must have discernment, because Christian love is not blind. In the Sermon on the Mount our Lord Jesus said, "Do not give dogs what is sacred; do not throw your pearls to pigs" (Matt. 7:6). This means we must exercise discernment if we're to know who the swine and the dogs are! Satan is a great imitator, and he has his wolves in sheep's clothing infiltrating the flock. We must not distribute the treasures of God's Word carelessly. We must exercise discernment.

However, if we aren't careful, we can turn discernment into a critical, judgmental attitude. In trying to be true to God, we may become so critical that we think we're the only ones who are right and that everybody else is wrong. We do have to exercise discernment, and that means knowing the Word, praying, and depending on the Holy Spirit. That's the first principle we must learn.

We Must Start with Ourselves

The second guideline is simply this: we must start with ourselves. The Bible doesn't forbid us to help others by pointing out their faults so long as we examine ourselves first. "Do not judge, or you too will be judged" (Matt. 7:1). If you stopped right there, you would conclude that it's always wrong to judge. But read the rest of the passage. "For in the same way as you judge others, you will be judged, and with the measure you use, it will be measured to you" (v. 2). In other words, we get back just what we give and in the measure we give. If we are critical of others, others will be critical of us.

Those of us who stand in the pulpit and proclaim the Word must remember that our people will become what we are. If we're judgmental and critical, they will be judgmental and critical. We must be very careful to share the truth in love and to bathe our messages in prayer.

"Why do you look at the speck of sawdust in your brother's eye and pay no attention to the plank in your own eye? Or how can you say to your brother, 'Let me take the speck out of your eye,' when all the time there is a plank in your own eye?" (vv. 3–4). The crowd must have laughed out loud when Jesus said this. Eastern people love humorous exaggeration, and the picture of a doctor with a plank in his eye trying to take a speck out of his patient's eye is absolutely ridiculous!

When I was in junior high school, I was playing soccer one day on the school field, and some building construction was going on nearby. A tiny piece of cement lodged in my eye, and I had to go see an eye specialist. I will never forget how she bent over me, put a special magnifying device over her eyes, and picked out that little piece of cement from my eye. It felt so good to get rid of it! But suppose there had been something in her own eye so that she couldn't see what she was doing?

Our Lord gave us a practical principle in Matthew 7: by all means, we should try to help our brothers and sisters, but we must start first with ourselves. "You hypocrite, first take the plank out of your own eye, and then you will see clearly to remove the speck from your brother's eye" (v. 5). We must exercise discernment, we should help our brothers and sisters, but we must begin by examining ourselves.

I have not always followed this principle, and I have suffered for it. I'm praying that God will help me to follow it faithfully. Before we criticize somebody else, we had better make sure there isn't something worse in our own life. When we deal first with ourselves, we'll be able to see other people's situations a lot more clearly and we'll have a great deal more compassion. I don't want an eye doctor operating on my eye with a crowbar and a pipe wrench! I want tenderness and compassion, because the eye is one of the most sensitive parts of the human body. So we don't rush up to people to condemn and judge. We first examine our own lives to see what we need to deal with. We must begin with ourselves.

Jesus Christ Is Lord!

One of the important guidelines Paul gave in Romans 14 is that we remember that Jesus Christ is Lord. He uses the word "Lord" at least ten times in the chapter. The Lord Jesus Christ may want to use us to help someone else, but Jesus alone is Lord. We must not play God in the lives of other people, for only Jesus Christ is Lord. "For this very reason, Christ died and returned to life so that he might be the Lord of both the dead and the living. You, then, why do you judge your brother? Or why do you look down on your brother?" (vv. 9–10). The weak Christians were judging the strong Christians, and the strong Christians were despising the weak ones. "For we will all stand before God's judgment seat" (v. 10).

I have no right to judge my brother as though I were the Lord Jesus. All of us have been judged by others in one way or another. Those of us who minister widely, by means of radio and in other ways, sometimes get very critical letters from people. We wonder sometimes if they have really prayed and thought the matter through. But we must remember that Jesus is Lord. I must never take the place of Jesus in somebody's life. I cannot do it. If I am going to pass judgment on you, I must first come to the Lord and let Him be the Lord of my life. I must say, "O Lord Jesus, You are God, You are the Judge. Now, if You want me to deal with my brother, show me from the Word and give me guidance by the Holy Spirit because I cannot do this myself." If I do it myself, certainly I am going to fail and cause trouble.

We Must Have Priorities

Paul laid down another guideline when he instructed us to have priorities in our lives and to deal only with things that are really important. "I am fully convinced that no food is unclean in itself" (Rom. 14:14). Under the Old Testament law, God specified clean and unclean foods for the Jewish nation. This was a part of God's training of His people in exercising spiritual discernment and learning to separate the holy and the unholy. When our Lord died and rose again, and when the Holy Spirit came, all these distinctions were erased; and today there is no such thing as clean or unclean food. Some food may not be good for you physically, but that's another matter. Concerning the spiritual consequences of what you eat, the Word of God makes it very clear that one kind of food is just like another. What goes into your stomach doesn't affect your spiritual life. (See Mark 7:1–23 and 1 Tim. 4:1–5.)

In the churches in Rome, the Christians with a weak conscience followed rules and regulations and were very legalistic in demanding that all the believers eat only clean foods. But the strong Christians, people who believed the Word of God and lived by grace, said, "Yes, we can eat everything. Jesus said so and so did Paul." And so there was a division. "But if any one regards something as unclean, then for him it is unclean. If your brother is distressed because of what you eat, you are no longer acting in love. Do not by your eating destroy your brother for whom Christ died. . . . Do not destroy the work of God for the

49

sake of food" (Rom. 14:14–15, 20). Some Christians make mountains out of molehills and fail to emphasize the really important things in life. They need priorities.

Perhaps you heard about the farmer who was out working in his field. He saw a mouse eating at his crops, and that so angered him that he took his hoe and began to go after that mouse. He spent the next thirty minutes chasing and beating at that mouse, and he finally killed him. Then he looked around and realized that he had wrecked an acre of his crops just to get rid of the mouse. Was it worth it? Probably not.

Having priorities is a mark of maturity. Some things are more important than other things, and to destroy a fellow Christian over the matter of eating and drinking is simply not worth it. To destroy a Sunday school class over which Bible translation to use is simply not worth it. To destroy a church over what kind of recreation or entertainment is acceptable is foolish. Paul said in Romans 14:21, "It is better not to eat meat or drink wine or to do anything else that will cause your brother to fall." The spiritual growth of a Christian brother or sister is important, especially if they are weak in the faith. But we must not destroy the work of God for the sake of our own prejudices and opinions. We must have priorities.

We Must Show Love and Patience

"We who are strong ought to bear with the failings of the weak and not to please ourselves. Each of us should please his neighbor for his good, to build him up" (Rom. 15:1–2). Notice that it says "for his good." We don't always please our children, because some of the things they want to do are not for their good. But as much as possible, the strong Christians (who are walking in the freedom of God's grace) ought to please the weak Christians so they can lovingly help them grow.

Parents and grandparents do this for the sake of their little ones. We adjust our schedules to that of the baby, and we adjust our plans to those of the school. We set aside our personal desires for the sake of our children and grandchildren. This is the only way they can grow up and be mature adults. The strong Christians in the fellowship must consider the weak Christians and not selfishly please themselves.

This means we need discernment, and we must start with ourselves when it comes to judging. We must have priorities and not destroy God's great work in somebody's life for something unimportant. We must show love and patience, and as much as possible, we must try to please the weaker Christians for their good.

It's not wrong to exercise judgment, but it is wrong to be judgmental and try to play God in somebody's life. It's not wrong to have discernment, but it is wrong to think that we're the only ones who are right. We must remember that Jesus Christ is Lord. Recognizing the lordship of Jesus Christ helps to solve so many problems. I think it's important that you and I forsake a judgmental attitude and help our Christian brothers and sisters to mature in the Lord. We must be tender and loving, patient and kind, and we must seek as much as possible to help one another grow.

Caring Christians don't judge one another.

7

Bear One
Another's Burdens

Caring Christians bear each other's burdens. "Brothers, if someone is caught in a sin, you who are spiritual should restore him gently. But watch yourself, or you also may be tempted. Carry each other's burdens, and in this way you will fulfill the law of Christ. If anyone thinks he is something when he is nothing, he deceives himself. Each one should test his own actions. Then he can take pride in himself, without comparing himself to somebody else, for each one should carry his own load" (Gal. 6:1–5).

There seems to be a contradiction between verse 2 and verse 5, but there isn't. In Galatians 6:2 the word for "burdens" refers to a heavy load, a trial, something that is very difficult to bear. In verse 5 the word refers to a little load you carry on your back. This word was used for a soldier's pack.

There are certain burdens in my life that only I can bear, responsibilities I can't delegate to others because I have to fulfill that work myself. I have to be the husband and the father in my home, and I have to do the work that God has called me to do. Therefore, I have to bear my own burden. Every soldier has to shoulder his own pack. People who try to give their responsibilities to somebody else are both losing a blessing and disobeying God. So verse 5 is talking about the responsibilities of ministry, but verse 2 is talking about the burdens of life that are heavy to carry, the trials that come to us as believers. The admonition is "Carry each other's burdens, and in this way you will fulfill the law of Christ." This admonition is in the context of restoring a fellow believer who has sinned. If someone in the church has been overtaken by a fault—he was tempted and failed—we don't bear his guilt, but we do help him bear the burden of the consequences, and we help to restore him.

There are many burdens in life that we can help people carry. One of the beautiful things about the fellowship of the local church is that we get to know each other and therefore can better assist one another. We can help one another materially, physically, and spiritually. There are many ways that we as Christians can help to bear burdens. The particular way that is emphasized in Galatians 6 is helping those who have stumbled and fallen.

Paul gives us three practical instructions in this paragraph. He explains what we should do: bear each other's burdens. Then he tells us why we should do it: because of the law of Christ, which is the law of love. Then he explains how we should do it: with meekness.

What We Should Do

The emphasis here is on the word "restore." "Brothers, if someone is caught in a sin, you who are spiritual should restore him gently" (Gal. 6:1).

Restoring, not rejoicing. The word "restore" is not the word "rejoice." It doesn't say you should rejoice if someone sins. Some people enjoy it when other Christians fall because they think it makes them look good. Yet when one member of the body hurts, it hurts all of us. The eye can't say, "I'm glad the tack is in the foot and not in me." But that tack in the foot might fester and get infected, and it could one day affect the eye! No believer can fall without it affecting other believers. Galatians 6:1 doesn't say to rejoice because somebody sinned.

Restoring, not revealing. We aren't called to tell the world about the sin of fellow believers. Some Christians enjoy hanging out dirty linen. When Noah got drunk and lay in his tent naked, his son Ham laughed at him and told the other two sons (see Gen. 9:20–23). But Shem and Japheth backed into the tent and covered their father, because "love covers a multitude of sins" (James 5:20; 1 Peter 4:8). Love doesn't cleanse sin; only the grace of God through the blood of Christ can do that. Love doesn't condone sin, because if you love someone, you want her or him to enjoy the will of God. There's no reason to hang dirty wash out in public.

Restoring, not rejecting. The Bible doesn't say "rejoice" or "reveal," nor does it say "reject." It doesn't say, "If somebody falls into sin, reject him, judge him, condemn him." The Pharisees did this, and this was wrong. The Bible says "restore." The doctors knew this word because it was a medical term used to describe the setting of a broken bone. The church is Christ's Body, and if a member of the church is out of the will of God and falls into sin, it's like having a broken bone. That bone has to be set. The only way to set a broken bone is with tenderness. If it isn't set properly, it is going to create problems. I have a friend who recently had to have his arm broken and reset because it hadn't been done properly a few years ago.

The fishermen knew this word because it meant "to mend the nets." It's translated that way in Matthew 4:21—"mending their nets." If nets aren't mended, they will start to tear, and then you can't use them. If Christians are not restored, God can't use them to catch "fish" and win the lost.

The soldiers knew this word; it meant "to equip an army." Unless we help to restore those who have sinned, they will never be able to win the battles of life. We aren't just restoring a brother or a sister, we're helping to equip a soldier to go out and fight the battle. One damaged soldier can make a local church lose the whole battle.

The sailors knew this word. It meant "to outfit a ship for a voyage." Each of us has to face the storms of life and carry some cargo to the glory of God. But if sinning Christians aren't restored, they can't safely make the voyage. We need to help them get rigged for the journey.

So, when we help to restore a wandering Christian, it's like setting a broken bone, mending torn nets, equipping an army, and outfitting a ship. That's what we're doing when we help another Christian return to fellowship with the Lord. We bear one another's burdens when we help to restore a believer who has failed. Do you know somebody who has sinned? Is there somebody in your church fellowship, your Sunday school class, your family who has gotten out of the will of God? What is your attitude toward that person? Are you rejoicing? Are you revealing his or her sin and telling everybody? Are you rejecting that person? God's Word says you should help to restore that person.

Why We Should Do It

"Carry each other's burdens, and in this way you will fulfill the law of Christ" (Gal. 6:2). We know what the law of Christ is: "A new commandment I give you: Love one another" (John 13:34). This command is repeated in one way or another over a dozen times in the New Testament. We don't restore people because of law; we do it because of love. Legalists don't know much about restoring people. A legalist has nothing to restore anybody with. The Pharisees were quick to judge and to condemn, but they had no love in their hearts. If someone did not meet their standards, they had nothing to do with that person.

Paul addressed his readers as brothers (Gal. 6:1). Restoring another Christian is a family matter. We love the members of our family and we care for the household of faith. "Therefore, as we have opportunity, let us do good to all people, especially to those who belong to the family of believers" (v. 10). When you love other believers, you help to restore them when they have sinned.

It's a wonderful thing to live by the law of love! The law of love takes care of all other laws because love is the fulfillment of the law (Rom. 13:8–10). We can help to restore a brother or sister if we have the love of Christ in our hearts. The way we treat those who have sinned is evidence of our own spiritual condition. Legalists condemn sinners, but mature believers who love Jesus Christ try to restore sinners.

How We Should Do It

"Restore him gently," says Galatians 6:1. Gentleness and meekness are not weakness. Meekness is power under control. The meek person is filled with the Holy Spirit, because meekness is one of the fruits of the Spirit (5:22–23). Our Lord said, "Blessed are the meek, for they will inherit the earth" (Matt. 5:5). The Greek word translated "meek" pictures a horse that has been broken and now can be ridden because its power is under control.

Let's go back to the medical illustration I mentioned before. When doctors set broken bones, they keep their power under control. They don't use crowbars or pipe wrenches to do the job! They're gentle and considerate, and they make sure the fractured bones aren't damaged more. Would you call doctors weak because they were gentle in their work?

"But watch yourself, or you also may be tempted" (Gal. 6:1). What we think of ourselves determines how we treat

57

other people. If we're proud of our spirituality, we'll be hard on other people; but if we're humble before the Lord and realize how weak we are, we'll be gentle. Our Lord said this in the so-called Golden Rule: "In everything, do to others what you would have them do to you" (Matt. 7:12). If you say, "I might have sinned and been the one needing restoration," then you'll treat people with meekness and gentleness. But if you say, "Well, that could never happen to me! I would never do a thing like that!" then you will only make the situation worse.

Pride is usually the hidden reason why we refuse to help brothers and sisters who have sinned. "If anyone thinks he is something when he is nothing, he deceives himself" (Gal. 6:3). "I don't need any help," says the proud legalist. "I would never do a thing like that!" Paul warned us that we had better have meekness because we may be the next one who is tempted and falls. The very thing I say I won't do usually turns out to be the very thing that I will do.

We have the privilege and joy of bearing each another's burdens. We can give our burdens to the Lord, but often He uses other Christians to help us bear them. When you bear burdens, you share blessings. Christians aren't burdens to each other any more than a child is a burden to a loving mother. Our Lord Jesus Christ has set the example for us. When He was ministering here on earth, Jesus helped to carry many different kinds of burdens, including the burden of our sins that He bore on the cross. If He bears our burdens for us, shouldn't we help to bear the burdens of others?

As we share the burdens of others, God helps us with our own burdens. In the pastoral ministry, as I have shared burdens with people, how good the Lord has been to help me with my own burdens and battles. "Carry each other's burdens, and in this way you will fulfill the law of Christ" (v. 2).

Christians who care are Christians who bear each other's burdens.

8

Serve One Another

Christians who care serve one another. "You, my brothers, were called to be free. But do not use your freedom to indulge the sinful nature; rather, serve one another in love. The entire law is summed up in a single command: 'Love your neighbor as yourself.' If you keep on biting and devouring each other, watch out or you will be destroyed by each other. . . . Since we live by the Spirit, let us keep in step with the Spirit. Let us not become conceited, provoking and envying each other" (Gal. 5:13–15, 25–26).

God's people can bite and devour one another, destroy one another, provoke one another, envy one another, or serve one another in love. It doesn't even sound like Paul was writing to Christian people, but he was. Paul wrote to people who had made a profession of faith in Jesus Christ and were a part of the churches in Galatia. He exhorted them to live as those who were free in the Spirit. "So I say, live by the Spirit, and you will not gratify the desires of the sinful nature" (v. 16).

One reason Christians battle one another and split churches and break people's hearts is because they don't know how to serve one another in love and in the power of the Holy Spirit.

Two Attitudes

There are at least sixteen references to the Holy Spirit in Paul's letter to the Galatians. Many of the believers in Galatia were trying to please God by keeping the law when they needed to yield to the power of the Holy Spirit who alone enables us to serve God acceptably. "Serve one another in love" (5:13) can't be obeyed in our own natural strength, because we want others to serve us. Paul contrasted two different attitudes that lead to two different kinds of life. One is the fleshly attitude that puts us above everybody else, and the other is the spiritual attitude that motivates us to serve others.

By nature the flesh isn't interested in serving, because our old nature is basically selfish. The old nature fights against the Holy Spirit and tries to make us disobey the Lord. "For the sinful nature desires what is contrary to the Spirit, and the Spirit what is contrary to the sinful nature. They are in conflict with each other, so that you do not do what you want" (v. 17). If I yield to the old sinful nature, then the flesh controls my life, and this will be evident in the way I treat others. But if I yield to the Spirit, then the Holy Spirit will control my life, and Jesus will be glorified by the way I treat other people. In love, I will serve others.

If the old nature controls us, then we provoke one another, envy one another, devour one another, and are consumed by one another. If the Holy Spirit controls us, then we will serve one another in love.

The Galatian churches were invaded by a group of false teachers we call "the Judaizers." Their theology was that God's people—Jews and Gentiles alike—had to obey the law in order to be good Christians. Paul wrote this letter to convince them otherwise. Paul was not lawless, but he knew that Christians were not under the law but under God's grace (Gal. 5:18; Rom. 6:14–18).

In Romans 6, 7, and 8, Paul deals with our relationship to the law and makes it very clear that the old nature knows no law but the new nature needs no law. There never was a law given that can change or control the old nature. When we try to live by obeying religious law, it brings out the worst in us, which explains why the Galatian believers were fighting each other so much. The new nature needs no law except "the law of the Spirit of life" (Rom. 8:1–3). Through the Holy Spirit, we produce fruit that glorifies God and "feeds" others. "But the fruit of the Spirit is love, joy, peace, patience, kindness, goodness, faithfulness, gentleness and self-control. Against such things there is no law" (Gal. 5:22–23). The old nature knows no law, and the new nature needs no law, because God's righteousness is produced in us by the Spirit of God as we walk in the Spirit.

Nobody can pass a law to produce fruit. If an orchard isn't bearing fruit, the city council or the state legislature can't pass a law that will cause the trees to produce. You don't pass laws to produce fruit, because fruit doesn't come from law— it comes from life. This is why the legalistic approach to the Christian life is all wrong. Legalistic people who say that you must obey this rule or that law in order to be spiritual are contradicting the Word of God.

Legalism, License, or Love?

Christians are not lawless. The law is their servant, not their master. In Jesus Christ, we are free from the law of Moses, but because we live in the Spirit, we don't use our freedom "to indulge the sinful nature" (Gal. 5:13) because we walk in love. Our obedience is motivated by love, not fear. When it comes to living the Christian life, we have three possibilities: legalism, license, or love.

Legalism means you live under the law and the law is your master. Paul makes it crystal clear in Galatians that this approach is definitely wrong. "It is for freedom that Christ has set us free. Stand firm, then, and do not let yourselves be burdened again by a yoke of slavery" (5:1). In His life on earth, Jesus Christ perfectly obeyed the law, and in His death on the cross, He bore the curse of the law and set us free from the law. Why should we want to exchange our glorious freedom for the yoke of slavery?

But the other extreme is license, and the people who live like this consider the law to be their enemy. "I can do what I please!" is their motto because they forget that Christians are supposed to live to please God, not themselves. "Do not use your freedom to indulge the sinful nature" (5:13). License means throwing off all restraint and deliberately breaking the law, but liberty means walking in the power of the Holy Spirit and fulfilling the righteousness of the law. Freedom is a wonderful blessing. Freedom turned upward means God is glorified. Freedom turned outward means I can serve you. But when freedom is turned inward, it becomes license, and this leads to bondage.

The Law of Love

Paul rejected both license and legalism and affirmed the law of love. "The entire law is summed up in a single command: 'Love your neighbor as yourself'" (Gal. 5:14). We've encountered this precious truth over and over again in our study of the "one another" statements in the New Testament. "Serve one another in love" (v. 13).

When you look at Galatians 5:15 and 5:26, you don't see much love, do you? The people were biting and devouring one another. They were competing against each other, seeing who could obey the law the best, and comparing levels of spirituality. The Judaizers said, "If you'll obey the law, then you'll be spiritual." The minute you have rules and regulations to obey, then you can start measuring yourself, and the

Christian life becomes easy. And when you start measuring yourself, you can also start measuring other people. We have four children, and each of them is different. It's impossible to measure one by the other. We can't say to the second child, "Well, you ought to be like your big brother." We can't say to the fourth child, "You ought to be like your sister." Each of them is different.

When Christians start to compare themselves with others, they have moved into legalism. They tend to measure spirituality quantitatively instead of qualitatively, and this is dangerous. You can't measure spirituality quantitatively any more than you can measure children quantitatively instead of qualitatively. The fact that one child is a foot taller than another child doesn't mean he is better than the other child. It just means he's taller, that's all. The Galatians began to bite and devour one another, provoke one another, and envy one another because they had stepped out of the realm of grace and moved into the bondage of law. Law always brings out the worst in us and creates the old problem of competition: Who is the most spiritual? It's the internal problem of flesh versus Spirit and the external problem of self versus others.

It's legalism or license versus true liberty in love. Where there is love, there can be freedom. The most liberating thing in life is love through the Holy Spirit. When you love others, you don't want to exploit them, compete with them, bite them, or devour them. According to verse 15, if we fight each other, we end up destroying each other. Some groups establish very rigid, legalistic rules, and they say, "Now we are going to be spiritual." Unfortunately, that doesn't happen because "the law of the Spirit of life in Christ Jesus" (Rom. 8:2) is the only law that can change and control our lives. The Holy Spirit of God, working in us and through us in love, enables us to "serve one another" (Gal. 5:13).

Our Lord Jesus Christ is the greatest example of this. The Pharisees criticized Him because He didn't keep their legalistic rules. He didn't stop His disciples from plucking and eating the grain in the fields on the Sabbath day (see Matt. 12:1–8). Jesus deliberately healed people on the Sabbath Day (see vv. 9–14), and the Pharisees were incensed over what He did. But our Lord served others in love and lived in the freedom of the Spirit.

Unless there is love in our hearts, we cannot render true service to others, because true Christian service is motivated by love. In Ephesians 6:6 Paul told the Christian servants to "do the will of God from [the] heart." They were not to do God's will out of a sense of duty but from the heart, from within. We're to serve one another in love because we delight in doing it, not because we have to do it. We must honestly ask ourselves, "Is my life governed by love? Do I serve others in love?"

"Called to Freedom"

We have been "called to be free" (Gal. 5:13) and Jesus Christ died to set us free, so that we can be servants of God and His people. We've not been called to freedom so we can enjoy ourselves and do as we please. Liberty is too precious for that. Do you know that your liberty in Jesus Christ cost Him His life on the cross? Liberty is a costly thing, whether it be political freedom or spiritual freedom. This liberty is so expensive it should not be abused. Why did God call us to freedom? That we might use that liberty to serve one another.

Sacrificial service in love is a mark of maturity. Mature people don't use their freedom selfishly; they use it for others. We would be wise to yield to the Holy Spirit of God and allow Him to produce the fruit of the Spirit in our lives, and the first fruit on that list is love: "The fruit of the Spirit is love" (v. 22). I believe that fullness of love produces joy; fullness of love and joy will produce peace; fullness of love, joy, and peace will produce longsuffering, and this will produce gentleness. One quality leads to the next one! Because of these blessed qualities of the Spirit-filled Christian life, we don't need laws, rules, and regulations to tell us how to live. When you are walking in the Spirit—"keeping in step with the Spirit"—the life of God within produces the fruit that glorifies God.

Are we filled with excessive pride? Do we compare and contrast ourselves with others? Are we guilty of measuring ourselves by ourselves and making other people look unspiritual so that we might look spiritual? Are we provoking and envying people? These are the marks of fleshly legalism or of using freedom in the wrong way. How much better it would be if we would just yield to the Holy Spirit and find freedom in the law of love—not in the law of Moses but in the law of love that fulfills all the law. "Serve one another in love" (v. 13).

May the Lord help each of us to be, not servants of sin, but servants of God's people, loving one another and serving one another.

Christians who care serve one another in love.

9

Forgive One Another

Caring Christians forgive one another. Ephesians 4:32 admonishes us, "Be kind and compassionate to one another, forgiving each other, just as in Christ God forgave you."

An unforgiving spirit creates all kinds of problems. In my pastoral ministry, I have counseled people who had physical difficulties, not because of sickness or injury, but because of hostile and bitter attitudes in their hearts. Psychiatrists have observed that people who have emotional problems often have interpersonal problems, usually an unforgiving spirit. This is why the Holy Spirit directed Paul to write: "And do not grieve the Holy Spirit of God, with whom you were sealed for the day of redemption. Get rid of all bitterness, rage and anger, brawling and slander, along with every form of malice. Be kind and compassionate to one another, forgiving each other, just as in Christ God forgave you."

Let's try to answer a few questions about this matter of family forgiveness. Paul was not writing about God's forgiveness when we trust Christ for salvation; he was writing about members of the Christian family forgiving one another.

Most believers have little difficulty forgiving unsaved people, but when it comes to forgiving members of the church family, that's a different matter.

Evidences of an Unforgiving Spirit

When Christians cultivate an unforgiving spirit, this is usually evidence that there are other sins harbored in the heart.

Unwholesome talk. The way we talk about other people reveals what we really have in our hearts, for it's out of the overflow of the heart that the mouth speaks (Matt. 12:34). Paul had a great deal to say about human speech. For example, he said in Ephesians 4:29, "Do not let any unwholesome talk come out of your mouths, but only what is helpful for building others up according to their needs, that it may benefit those who listen."

When we cultivate an unforgiving spirit, we say things about people that we shouldn't say. In verse 31 Paul wrote about "bitterness" and "malice," two sins that help produce sinful speech. If I'm the kind of person who immediately jumps at the chance to say something evil about somebody, that means I'm holding a grudge against that person. One of the first evidences of an unforgiving spirit is saying critical and slanderous things about people. If we can't say something good, it usually means that there's something sinful lurking in our own hearts.

Poisoned emotions. Another evidence of an unforgiving spirit is bad feelings within us toward others. Perhaps we're able to control our tongues and not say evil things about people, but our friends would be shocked if they could see the poisoned feelings we have down inside, feelings like bitterness and anger. Somebody hurts us, and instead of getting the misunderstanding straightened out, we get bitter and refuse to forgive. Bitterness is to the heart what an infection is to the body: it spreads poison and does great damage.

One summer when I was just a young boy, I was plagued with boils. They really hurt! What that infection was to my body, bitterness is to my heart. Some Christians hold things inside, and the bitterness just grows like an infection in the system. When you have a serious infection, your body becomes very sensitive and everything hurts. Bitterness is evidence of an unforgiving spirit. So are wrath, anger, and clamor. When there's a fever in the body, it's difficult to hide it; and when there's bitterness in the heart, you can't hide it. When the person we dislike is mentioned, we get angry and often decide to say something that we shouldn't say.

Unwholesome talk, evil speaking, bitterness, rage, anger, and malice are evidences of an unforgiving spirit. Malice is that hateful feeling that we nurture down inside. How easy it is to lie in bed at night and to think up all sorts of evil things about those who have wronged us! That is another evidence of an unforgiving spirit.

When we have this kind of attitude, are we hurting the other person? Of course not! If someone has done something to me I didn't like, and if I'm harboring resentment, am I hurting the person who offended me? No, I'm only hurting myself. Having an unforgiving spirit is like maintaining a disease that can easily be cured: you are only hurting yourself.

A church member came to me one day and said, "Pastor Wiersbe, I want to apologize to you."

"For what?" I asked.

"Well," she said, "I've had some terrible attitudes toward you and I'm sorry."

"I appreciate your apology," I said, "but the matter is really between you and God. Your bad attitudes didn't hurt me, they hurt you."

If she had done something outwardly, like criticizing me or slandering me, that would have been a different story. But she had these unkind feelings in her heart and I knew nothing about them. The lady was hurting only herself. Unkind words, evil words, and bitter thoughts and feelings down

69

inside are all evidences of an unforgiving spirit, but an unfor-giving spirit can be forgiven!

Essentials for a Forgiving Spirit

I don't think any believer really wants to cultivate an unforgiving heart. We appreciate it when others forgive us, and we know that we should forgive others. People who won't forgive others are destroying the very bridge over which they themselves may have to walk someday. If we don't forgive others, we're putting a barrier between us and other people and between us and God. In fact, our Lord Jesus said that forgiving our brother is one of the conditions for answered prayer (see Matt. 6:15).

Kindness. One essential for a forgiving spirit is kindness. "Be kind and compassionate to one to another" (Eph. 4:32). In Ephesians 2:7 Paul wrote about God's kindness in our sal-vation: "In order that in the coming ages he [God] might show the incomparable riches of his grace, expressed in his kindness to us in Christ Jesus." Stop and consider the kind-ness of God toward us. Titus 3 describes what we were like before we were saved: "At one time we too were foolish, dis-obedient, deceived and enslaved by all kinds of passions and pleasures. We lived in malice and envy, being hated and hat-ing one another" (v. 3). If we had stayed like that, we would have been condemned forever. But Paul went on to say, "But when the kindness and love of God our Savior appeared, he saved us, not because of righteous things we had done, but because of his mercy" (vv. 4–5). Were it not for God's mercy and kindness, we would not be saved.

Second Samuel 9 provides a beautiful illustration of the kindness of God toward undeserving people. David the king asked his officers, "Is there anybody left in the house of Saul to whom I can show kindness for Jonathan's sake?" What is "the kindness of God"? It's kindness that is lavished on those who are undeserving. Had Saul done anything good for David? No, yet David said, "I want to show God's kindness to somebody in the house of Saul." David's officers found Mephibosheth, a crippled man who was the son of Jonathan, and David showed him kindness because of Jonathan. That is the kindness of God. David made this man a prince in his household and gave him everything he needed, and he did it for the sake of another.

God is kind to us, not because we're good but for the sake of Jesus Christ, His beloved Son. Because of the grace of the Lord Jesus Christ, we're children of God today. If I am going to have a forgiving heart, I must realize the kindness of God and seek to imitate it. We don't forgive because people deserve it, but because God forgave us—and we didn't deserve it. The kindness of God is always shown to those who are undeserving.

A tender heart. A hard heart is a terrible thing to have beating in your breast. When you have a hard heart, it robs you of blessing and joy. A hard heart is the result of bitterness, anger, wrath, and malice that haven't been confessed and washed away. A hard heart forms when we harbor evil feelings and refuse to show love to others. Paul said that if we are tenderhearted, then we can forgive (see Eph. 4:32).

Honesty. A third essential for a forgiving spirit is honesty. In Ephesians 4:15 Paul urged us to speak the truth in love. In Matthew 18 our Lord gave us instructions on how to get along with each other. If a Christian brother or sister sins against you, go and tell the person privately. Don't make a big scene; just seek reconciliation. If the person won't listen to you, take one or two other believers along to help you; and if the offender won't listen to them, take it to the church (Matt. 18:15–17). My experience as a pastor has been that when we take that first step, God usually works in the person's heart, and the problem gets solved.

It's wonderful when saints are honest with each other in love. If someone in your church fellowship has done something against you, don't go around talking about it, don't cultivate bitterness, and don't develop a hard heart. Instead of thinking up unkind things to say and do to retaliate, go to the person honestly and humbly and try to get the matter settled. Do you know why? Because God forgave you in Christ (Eph. 4:32).

At the end of Matthew 18 our Lord told the parable about the servant who owed the king a great deal of money, and the king ordered him and his family to be sold so that the debt could be paid. But the man begged and said, "Please give me time." The king took pity on him and forgave him the entire debt. Then the servant met a friend who owed him a small amount of money. He grabbed him by the throat and shook him and said, "Pay what you owe me!" The friend begged him to be patient, saying, "I'll pay if you'll give me time." But he wouldn't give him time nor would he forgive him. When the king heard about this, he was very angry, and he put the servant into prison because he had not forgiven his fellow servant.

An unforgiving spirit will put you into an emotional and spiritual prison every single time. If you don't forgive your brother or your sister, it will make a prisoner out of you, a prisoner of bitterness and anger, a prisoner of malice. What an agonizing way to live! The freedom of forgiveness is a marvelous thing. God has forgiven us, and so we are free to forgive others. Why do we forgive others? Because God has forgiven us.

Often I hear people say, "Well, I can forgive, but I can't forget." The Bible doesn't say that we forget all the painful things that people have done. In the Bible "to forget" means "not to hold it against a person." When God says, "For I will forgive their wickedness and will remember their sins no more" (Heb. 8:12), it does not mean He actually forgets something that happened. God cannot forget anything. It simply means He doesn't hold against us the sins we've confessed to Him and asked Him to forgive.

I remember bad things that people have done to me and said about me, but the pain of these offenses is gone, along with whatever bitterness may have been there. I have forgiven them, and I don't hold their sins against them anymore. If I meet them, what happened between us no longer stands in the way.

Other people say, "But it's so hard to forgive!" That may be true, but it's even harder *not to forgive!* If we don't forgive, we grieve the Holy Spirit and deny what Jesus did for us on the cross. If we don't forgive, we're not walking in love. Ephesians 5:2 says, "And live a life of love, just as Christ loved us and gave himself up for us."

Caring Christians forgive one another. Life is too short to have enemies, and enemies are very expensive. We will forgive one another, not because anybody deserves it, but for Jesus' sake.

Christians who care forgive one another.

10

Submit to One Another

Christians who care submit themselves to one another. "Submit to one another out of reverence for Christ" (Eph. 5:21). "Young men, in the same way be submissive to those who are older. All of you, clothe yourselves with humility toward one another, because, 'God opposes the proud but gives grace to the humble'" (1 Peter 5:5).

We're living in an era of self-expression and independence. The slogan of many people seems to be, "I'm going to do my thing my way, and don't try to stop me!" Yet the Word of God tells us that the way to personal fulfillment isn't through asserting ourselves but through submitting ourselves. Yet this must be a submission that comes from the fullness of the Holy Spirit. "Do not get drunk on wine, which leads to debauchery. Instead, be filled with the Spirit" (Eph. 5:18).

But how can you tell if people are really filled with the Holy Spirit? Do they perform miracles? Do they have a strange glow on their faces? According to Paul, there are three evidences of the fullness of the Holy Spirit.

We are joyful. "Speak to one another with psalms, hymns and spiritual songs. Sing and make music in your heart to the Lord" (v. 19).

We are thankful. "Always giving thanks to God the Father for everything, in the name of our Lord Jesus Christ" (v. 20).

We are submissive. "Submit to one another out of reverence for Christ" (v. 21).

This whole matter of submission, then, relates to the fullness of the Holy Spirit.

If you and I are walking in the power of the flesh, we will not submit to the Lord or to His people. The flesh is proud and always wants to assert itself. The New Testament has nothing good to say about the flesh. "The flesh counts for nothing" (John 6:63). "I know that nothing good lives in me, that is, in my sinful nature" (Rom. 7:18). If we walk in the Holy Spirit's power, then we will be joyful, thankful, and submissive.

Please don't reverse that order! We first submit to the Holy Spirit and let Him fill us, because to be filled with the Holy Spirit means to be controlled by the Holy Spirit. The Holy Spirit then thinks through our minds, loves through our hearts, and acts through our wills, using the members of our bodies to serve and glorify Christ. The result of that filling is that we are joyful, thankful, and submissive.

When Christians are joyful, they have no problem submitting to others. But when we complain, criticize, and think we've been mistreated, then we have a hard time submitting. We start asserting ourselves to get what we think we really deserve.

Submission must not be confused with subjugation or slavery. We're not talking about bondage; we're talking about freedom. In the local church or in the home, there's no place for bondage because we've been called into the gracious liberty that belongs to God's children. However, this liberty means freedom to submit to one another. Perhaps a good illustration is the human body. My body is made up of many different members. Each member has a function to perform, but each member depends upon the other members. As the members of my body submit to one another, the body functions normally. I feel good, and I get my work done. But suppose one member of my body decides not to submit and wants to go its own way. Then I have trouble and I may have to go to the doctor. I might even need surgery to correct what is wrong.

We want to apply this principle of submission in three different areas of life. First, we consider our submission to God, because the church is subject to Christ (Eph. 5:24) Second, we consider our submission in marriage and the home. Ephesians 5:22 commands wives to submit to their husbands "as to the Lord." Verse 25 commands husbands to love their wives "just as Christ loved the church." Finally, we consider our submission to one another in the church. Ephesians 5:21 says, "Submit to one another out of reverence for Christ."

Submission to God

It all begins with submission to the Lord, for the church "submits to Christ" (Eph. 5:24). The church collectively must be subject to Christ because Christ is the head of the church, but believers must be personally and individually submitted to the Lord and obey His will. The classic text on surrender to the Lord is Romans 12:1–2: "Therefore, I urge you, brothers, in view of God's mercy, to offer your bodies as living sacrifices, holy and pleasing to God—this is your spiritual act of worship. Do not conform any longer to the pattern of this world, but be transformed by the renewing of your mind. Then you will be able to test and approve what God's will is—his good, pleasing and perfect will."

The first step in submitting to the Lord is to give Him your body. He made our bodies His temple when we trusted Christ and the Holy Spirit came to dwell with us. He also wants our minds so that He might renew them and enable us to think as He wants us to think. The Word commands us not to be conformed to this world but to be transformed. He also wants our wills so that we'll obey Him and learn to enjoy His will.

If you want to practice submission, I suggest that every morning you give God your body, your mind, and your will. Ask the Holy Spirit to fill you. That's the beginning of a life of daily victory. Take time to read the Word and meditate on what it says, and the Lord will transform your mind. Then pray to the Lord and ask Him to guide you during the day and to help you obey His will. This is the way to begin the day as a submitted Christian.

Submission in the Home

If we are submitted to the Lord, we'll have no problem submitting in the home. Whether we're single or married, each of us has some family relationship. It's too bad that many families are being destroyed today by selfishness and sin. Satan is using his most destructive forces against the home, and too many families invite him in by means of television, the Internet, or computer games. One of these destructive forces is the selfish independence of people who say, "I'm going to go my way!"

It's tragic to watch homes being destroyed by sin. It usually happens this way. A home is founded, and the husband and wife make loving promises to each other and to the Lord. They promise to love, honor, obey, and submit. Then somewhere along the line, one of the partners decides he or she wants to go an independent way. The slogan today is "I'm doing it my way!" One of the partners then goes off and tries

78

to make it alone, breaking the vows made to God and to the other partner.

If there's going to be happiness and holiness in the home, there has to be submission. This is not subjugation, slavery, or bondage, not dictatorship but headship, a living, loving relationship between husband and wife. The partners must submit to one another. If a husband is submitted to the Lord and a wife is submitted to the Lord, they have no problem submitting to each other. The wife shows her submission by her obedience, and the husband shows his submission by his love. The wise husband knows the strengths of his wife and gives her freedom to use her gifts to build the home, and the loving wife accepts the strengths of her husband and submits to his direction.

You may ask, "Why didn't Paul say something about the husband's submitting?" He did! "Submit to one another out of reverence for Christ" (Eph. 5:21). But in verse 25 he pointed out that the husband has a greater responsibility in that he is supposed to love his wife "just as Christ loved the church." Jesus submitted to the ultimate obedience, "even death on a cross" (Phil. 2:8). That's submission! The husband's love is to be a sacrificial love, not a demanding love.

Where these commandments are obeyed and the principle of loving submission is followed, the home will experience the blessing of God. Once again, this mutual submission is not slavery or subjugation. It's the freedom that comes from submitting first to the Lord and then lovingly to a mate who is filled with the Holy Spirit. Would any wife have a problem submitting to a husband who is joyful, thankful, and submitted to the Lord? I think not.

Submission in the Local Church

The third area of submission is in the local church. As both a former pastor and now an itinerant Bible teacher, it's been my privilege to teach the Word of God in hundreds of churches in different parts of the world. It's a great joy to find churches made up of people who are submitted to the Lord and to one another. Too often, however, people in churches debate with one another, disagree, and fight with one another. Some churches split, and the splits produce splinters, and the testimony of the Lord is hurt.

The principle of submission in the church is described in 1 Peter 5: "Be shepherds of God's flock that is under your care, serving as overseers—not because you must, but because you are willing, as God wants you to be; not greedy for money, but eager to serve; not lording it over those entrusted to you, but being examples to the flock" (vv. 2–3). There's no place in the church for a dictator, a "church boss" who tells everybody what to do.

"Young men, in the same way be submissive to those who are older. All of you, clothe yourselves with humility toward one another" (v. 5). That phrase reminds me of John 13, where the Lord Jesus put on the towel and washed the disciples' feet. "Clothe yourselves with humility." Why? Because "God opposes the proud but gives grace to the humble" (v. 5).

It's too bad that we sometimes have a few sanctified obstructionists on church boards who must always have their own way. Submission in the local church is the way for the church to grow and for God's blessing to come on His people. It is the way for the Holy Spirit to fill us and to work through all of us, old and young alike. When older saints and younger saints are submitted to the Lord and to each other, and learn from each other and when church leaders and church members, pastors, and people are submitted to the Lord and to one another, then the Spirit is free to bless abundantly.

Let me explain why submission is so important. It is important because when we're submitted, then God can control our lives. If we don't submit, then selfishness controls our lives, and that gives a foothold to the devil. People who say, "I'm going to do it my way" spend much of their time responding and reacting to the resistance of other people, and all the while they think they're controlling their own lives! When we submit, God controls; when we don't submit, then other people control. When we refuse to submit, we lead a defensive life of misery that can lead to battles and bondage. That's not the kind of life God wants us to live.

"Submit to one to another out of reverence for Christ" (Eph. 5:21). Are you a submissive Christian? Submissiveness doesn't mean we lose ourselves; it means that we find ourselves and the ministry the Lord has for us. Submission doesn't mean that God cheats us; rather, it means that God enriches us.

Caring Christians submit to one another out of reverence for Christ.

11

Prefer One Another

Christians who care prefer one another in honor. "Love must be sincere. Hate what is evil; cling to what is good. Be devoted to one another in brotherly love. Honor one another above yourselves" (Rom. 12:9–10).

Everyone likes to receive recognition. We all like to be appreciated. Certainly there's nothing wrong with honest recognition and appreciation. In fact, Paul wrote to the Thessalonians and told them to know their spiritual leaders and respect them, and to honor them for the work they had done (1 Thess. 5:12–13). God must always receive the glory, but God's servants deserve honor.

But the admonition of Romans 12:9–10 tells us that we should prefer one another in honor. That simply means you and I should be willing for others to get the recognition and to receive the honor even though we may be left out. We should be willing to go unrecognized if this is the will of God. Christians are to prefer one another in honor.

I want to look at two aspects of this statement: first, what it doesn't mean and, second, what it does mean and how we can put it into practice.

What Preferring One Another Does Not Mean

If we don't understand the meaning of this admonition, we may end up disobeying the Lord instead of growing in the Lord.

It does not mean empty flattery. Books are available these days that tell you how to flatter your way into or out of anything. There is a brand of popular psychology that tells you how to find the "hot button" in a person's life—what she or he is really interested in—and use that knowledge to your own advantage. A best-selling book tells you how to use compliments and praise to influence people to do what you want them to do. This leads, of course, to manipulating people, something that Christians must never do. Paul wasn't writing about empty flattery because in Romans 12:9 he warned us to be sure our love is sincere and without hypocrisy.

There is a hypocritical kind of love that is shallow and "gushy"—all words but no deeds. There is a kind of love that is manufactured, artificial, brittle, and very temporary. "Your love is like the morning mist, like the early dew that disappears" (Hos. 6:4). Paul tells us that our love for one another should be sincere and honest, without hypocrisy and flattery.

It's important in ministry that we sincerely love people and not use psychological tricks to influence people. Paul wrote to the Thessalonian believers, "You know we never used flattery, nor did we put on a mask to cover up greed— God is our witness" (1 Thess. 2:5). Paul and his associates didn't try to flatter people into the kingdom or to get something out of them. He was a faithful minister, not a flattering manipulator.

Some sermons I've heard were very manipulative. The preacher didn't expound and apply God's Word; he just told the people how wonderful they were and how fortunate the Lord was that they were in His church. It was only flattery, and God can't bless that kind of ministry. In fact, God warned against flattering lips. "A lying tongue hates those it hurts, and a flattering mouth works ruin" (Prov. 26:28). God hates flattery and God's people ought to avoid it. "Honor one another above yourselves" does not mean that we go around flattering each other.

It does not mean belittling ourselves. Some people have the idea that preferring others above ourselves means that we have to lie about ourselves and belittle ourselves. These people go around saying, "I can't do anything" or "I'm not worth anything." That kind of speech is sin because we're made in the image of God and saved by God's grace, and therefore in Christ we are worth something. Every believer has spiritual gifts from God that should be used for God's glory. Romans 12:3 warns us not to think of ourselves more highly than we ought to think, because that's pride. Instead, we ought to see ourselves honestly and sincerely. We want to avoid two extremes: thinking too highly of ourselves or thinking too lowly of ourselves.

When God called Moses, Moses belittled himself and told God he couldn't do anything. Moses said, "I am not an eloquent speaker; I am slow of speech" (see Exod. 4:10). God rebuked him and said, "I made your tongue and your mouth. Now you obey Me!" (see vv. 11–12). Belittling yourself means belittling God. Some people go to God's house and say, "I'm not very important at church. I don't teach a Sunday school class, I'm not on the church board, I don't sing in the choir, so I'm not very important." But you *are* important! Each believer is important to God.

In Romans 12:4–8, Paul pointed out that all Christians are members of the Body of Christ and all have gifts for service. We are members of one another (see vv. 4–5). When you belittle yourself, you're also belittling the other members of the Body, because we belong to each other. Our spiritual gifts differ (v. 6), but each gift is important because an all-wise God apportioned them to us. We must not belittle ourselves, but neither should we overestimate ourselves. Rather, we should see ourselves honestly and use the gifts God has given us for the benefit of the whole church.

If someone asks you to help in vacation Bible school or the summer camping program and you are able to help, you should do so. But if you say, "I can't do anything," that's not humility—it's a very subtle form of pride. You want them to reply, "But you can do so many things! We know what a good worker you are." "Honor one another above yourselves" doesn't mean empty flattery or belittling yourself. We must admit and accept the gifts God has given us and use them to build the church and glorify the Lord.

It does not mean showing partiality. We all tend to show partiality in one way or another. Even as parents and grandparents, we sometimes show partiality to our children and grandchildren. Leaders have a tendency to like the work of certain people, and most of us show partiality even among our friends. But when it comes to God's family, we have to be very careful not to show partiality. When Paul wrote to Timothy to instruct him about leading the local church, he admonished him "to keep these instructions without partiality" and "to do nothing out of favoritism" (1 Tim. 5:21). Paul admonished this young pastor to see all believers as members of the same family, each with a different ministry to perform.

This is a difficult rule to practice. I've pastored three churches, and I know that, in the local church, some people are very cooperative and some are not. It's very easy to be partial to the hardworking, cooperative people. But we must be careful not to show partiality. "Honor one another above yourselves" doesn't mean that we prefer one and hurt another. It doesn't mean that we get so wrapped up in one person that we neglect others.

In choosing officers and appointing workers, pastors and boards must be careful and prayerful, seeking the mind of the Lord. We must identify the spiritual gifts people have and try to make the best use of those gifts. All of us are in Christ, and this means that the externals—such as income, education, social position, race, or vocation—are secondary.

What Preferring One Another Does Mean

"Honor one another above yourselves" (Rom. 12:10) simply means putting other people ahead of ourselves when we have a choice to make. This is so easy to say and so hard to do!

This was one of the problems in the church at Philippi. Paul wrote to them in Philippians 2:3, "Do nothing out of selfish ambition or vain conceit, but in humility consider others better than yourselves." That word "better" means "more important." We must esteem other people more important than ourselves. Other people have greater talents than I do in certain areas. I'm not an athlete or a mechanic. I'm not a painter and I can't fix things. I have to admit that other people are better in those areas than I am, so I have no problem letting them step ahead of me.

But that's not what Paul was talking about. He's not instructing us to step aside in matters for which we're not gifted—even unsaved people can do that—but to step aside in *areas where we are gifted.* We must recognize our own gifts and abilities and use them for the Lord, but we must always be ready to let others with the same gifts go ahead of us. If we're motivated by selfish ambition and want to be "important" in the church, or if we have an inflated view of our abilities, then we'll create problems and cause division. But if we accept our gifts and let the Lord put us where He wants us, we'll build the church and be a blessing to others.

Someone has said that the way to have joy in the Christian life is to put Jesus first, others second, and yourself last; and that spells J-O-Y. This attitude demands love, which is why Paul wrote in Romans 12:10, "Be devoted to one another in brotherly love" and followed it with "Honor one another above yourselves." When you love someone, you

87

want that person to be in the place of honor and you aren't envious.

Consider the story of Abraham and Lot as recorded in Genesis 13. Their flocks and herds had multiplied, there had been a famine in the land, and consequently there wasn't enough pasture for all of their animals. Abraham and Lot learned that their herdsmen were fighting between themselves to get the best land. Abraham could have said to his nephew, "Now, Lot, I'm older than you so I am in charge." But Abraham didn't say that. Rather, he said, "Lot, if you go to the left, I'll go to the right; if you go to the right, I'll go to the left" (see v. 9). He preferred to give the honor to Lot. Lot abused that privilege, but that wasn't Abraham's fault. Abraham showed the right spirit in giving Lot first choice, but God had given all the land to Abraham anyway! When you walk by faith and believe God's promises, you have no problem putting others first.

This is where King Saul got into trouble. God began to use David as a mighty warrior in battle, and the Jewish women began to sing his praises, "Saul has slain his thousands, and David his tens of thousands" (1 Sam. 18:7). Saul became envious of David instead of giving thanks for his ability. Saul began to watch David, and before long envy turned to hatred and he tried to kill David! Saul's envy finally led to his ruin, and David became his successor.

It's very important that you and I have a right relationship to other believers and be willing to give honor where honor is due. We should show respect where respect is due. There is no competition in the work of the Lord because we belong to each other and we need each other. If we do our work to the glory of Jesus Christ, that's all that really counts.

Let's make this very practical. I have been in church services where people have stopped the pastor and asked, "Why did you announce the Sunday school class meeting but didn't announce our committee meeting?" The poor pastor was caught between two different ministries, both of them important. Perhaps somebody's name was left out of the worship folder, and as a result, that forgotten church member lost his or her joy that day. In our local churches, if we would pray, "Lord, help me to do my work diligently, and it doesn't matter who gets the honor, as long as You get the glory," what a difference it would make. Whenever you find people looking for recognition and praise in the church family, you have problems and potential divisions. We should be like John the Baptist, who said, "He [Jesus] must become greater; I must become less" (John 3:29–30).

So the next time we have the opportunity to let somebody else be first in line, we need to let them do it. The next time we have the opportunity to let some other believer receive recognition and appreciation, let's encourage it. Let's not sit back and say, "Well, I work harder than he does; somebody should surely recognize me." Instead, let's say, "Thank You, Father, for this fellow Christian and for the hard work he does. I pray that You will bless him abundantly." May there not be in our hearts that terrible poison of envy, strife, jealousy, and competition. Rather, may we practice what Paul instructed in Romans 12:10—"Honor one another above yourselves."

Caring Christians don't promote themselves. Caring Christians prefer one another in honor.

12

Show Hospitality to One Another

Christians who care show hospitality to one another without grumbling. "The end of all things is near. Therefore be clear minded and self-controlled so that you can pray. Above all, love each other deeply, because love covers over a multitude of sins. Offer hospitality to one another without grumbling" (1 Peter 4:7–9).

Often we forget that hospitality is a gift from God and a ministry to the Lord and to His people. Those wonderful people in our churches who open their hearts and homes to others are exercising a spiritual gift.

Over these more than fifty years of ministry, it's been my privilege to travel to many places to share the Word. How I thank God for those people who used their gift of Christian hospitality and welcomed me into their family circle! I have experienced true Christian love and generosity in homes in many parts of the world. Even today, my wife and I have dear friends in many places, people who used their gift of hospitality to meet our needs.

I'm grateful, too, that my wife and I have had the privilege of sharing Christian hospitality in our own home. Our four children have grown up expecting guests to be there, sometimes unexpectedly. We enjoy it and our family has been enriched by it. I wonder if old-fashioned Christian hospitality is perhaps on the wane in this present era when it's easier to put guests up in a motel. Use your home as a place of ministry to serve God. That's one reason He gave it to you. "Offer hospitality to one another without grumbling" (1 Peter 4:9).

Hospitality Is an Important Ministry

I want to deal with several facts in reference to this matter of hospitality. The first fact is this: Christian hospitality is an important ministry. We have a tendency to think that the "platform people" in church—the people who preach and sing—are doing the really important work for the Lord. One of the church's most important, although unseen, ministries is performed in the home: the ministry of hospitality.

A qualification for leadership. When Paul gave the qualifications for spiritual leaders in the local church, he mentioned hospitality (1 Tim. 3:2). This means that hospitality is important to the ministry of the pastor and elder. This same qualification is repeated in Titus 1:8. God expects Christian leaders to open their homes and share hospitality with others. I realize that in larger churches it's difficult for the leaders to have everybody in their home, but we should practice hospitality as much as possible and set a good example for others.

An opportunity for every believer. Hospitality is important not only to the spiritual leaders of the church but also to each member of the church. All of us have the privilege and responsibility of sharing our homes with others. "Practice hospitality" (Rom. 12:13) was written to all the members of the Body in the local church. The pastor and his wife aren't the only ones who should open their home to others, but all the church family should practice hospitality.

The phrase "Practice hospitality" means that hospitality should be habitual and not just occasional, when it's convenient. Hospitality isn't an obligation so much as an opportunity. We should devote ourselves to it, as it were, to become addicted to it. For the glory of God and the encouragement of His people, we should share what we have.

God has established only three institutions in this world: human government, the church, and the home. When God performed the first marriage and brought Adam and Eve together in Eden, He founded the first home. The Christian home should be a haven on earth. Charles Haddon Spurgeon once said, "When home is ruled according to God's word, angels might be asked to stay with us, and they would not find themselves out of their element." I wonder if the angels of God would feel comfortable in our homes today? Home is a place of ministry where we can glorify the Lord and serve Him.

One verse we usually think of in terms of hospitality is Hebrews 13:2—"Do not forget to entertain strangers, for by so doing some people have entertained angels without knowing it." Abraham is an example of this (see Gen. 18). One day while Abraham was resting, he saw three men coming down the road and he didn't know who they were. Later on he found out he had entertained our Lord and two of His angels. Abraham entertained angels unawares!

The word "angels" in the Greek text simply means "messengers." Did you ever stop to think that a guest in your home could be God's messenger to you and your family? I remember times when guests in our home proved to be the messengers of God by the blessings they brought with them.

Let me share just one instance from my own life. When I was in my first pastorate in northern Indiana, we entertained a wonderful Christian pastor who came to our church for a Bible conference. He was with us for less than a week and lived right in our home. My wife and I were a young married couple at the time, living in an upstairs apartment. It wasn't very fancy, but our guest made himself right at home. He was like a father to us during those brief days. Little did I realize how God would use that man in my life. A few years later, he contacted me to see if I might come and unite my ministry with his in the church that he was pastoring. We did, and then when God called him Home, I became pastor of that church. That pastor was a messenger of God in our home, and we have been blessed, and are still being blessed, because of that experience.

To be hospitable is important for the sake of the people in your family. Your children will be blessed if you are given to hospitality. You may say, "But we don't have a great deal to offer." That's not the point. Any person who loves God and who comes to your home is happy to be there regardless of what you have to offer. After all, you're not out to impress people but to bless people and show them the love of God.

Hospitality Was Vital in the Early Church

There were exceptions, but generally speaking, the people in the early church were not wealthy. When persecution began, the believers fled from one place to another, and the only refuge they could find was in the homes of God's people. The Christians opened their homes to not only the persecuted saints, but also the traveling preachers.

In 3 John 5–8 we have a glimpse of this.

> Dear friend, you are faithful in what you are doing for the brothers, even though they are strangers to you. They have told the church about your love. You do well to send them on their way in a manner worthy of God. It was for the sake of the Name that they went out, receiving no help from the pagans. We ought therefore to show hospitality to such men so that we may work together for the truth.

John was writing about the traveling preachers and evangelists who ministered from place to place and needed food and lodging. Gaius, the man who received this letter, opened his home to these servants of God. John told Gaius he was doing a faithful work and was a fellow-helper for the truth. You and I can help send out the truth by showing hospitality and taking care of those who minister.

Many of the early Christian assemblies met in homes, and when the service was over, some of the people had no place to go, so they just stayed! Wouldn't it be an interesting experience to have the entire congregation just stay right with you! Hospitality was a very important part of the ministry of the early church, and it should be important to Christians today.

Christian Hospitality Can Bring Blessing

Finally, let me remind you that Christian hospitality can be a source of blessing. "Give, and it will be given to you" (Luke 6:38). When we open our hearts, our hands, and our homes, God pours out His blessing. He multiplies His blessings when we share generously with others. That's why Peter wrote, "Offer hospitality to one another without grumbling" (1 Peter 4:9). Don't complain about it! We are stewards of God's grace (v. 10), and we must use what God has given to us to serve others. We are stewards not only of our spiritual gifts and our wealth but also of our home, and we must use our homes for God's glory. We are stewards of the money in our pockets and the food in our kitchens, and we should use what God has given to us for His glory. God always blesses those who are unselfish and who share what they have with others.

One of the statements of our Lord relating to hospitality is Matthew 25:35–36. I realize there are some prophetic overtones to this section, but there is a practical application as well. "For I was hungry and you gave me something to eat, I was thirsty and you gave me something to drink, I was a stranger and you invited me in, I needed clothes and you clothed me. I was sick and you looked after me." When asked how this ministry could have happened, the Lord replies, "I tell you the truth, whatever you did for one of the least of these brothers of mine, you did for me" (v. 40). When we share what we have with God's people, we are sharing it with Jesus Christ.

Caring Christians offer hospitality to one another without grumbling.

13

Do Not Lie
to One Another

Christians who care will not lie to one another. "Do not lie to each other, since you have taken off your old self with its practices and have put on the new self, which is being renewed in knowledge in the image of the Creator" (Col. 3:9–10).

God takes our words seriously. One day in the future, believers are going to stand before the Judgment Seat of Christ, and every idle word is going to come up for examination. The Ninth Commandment says, "You shall not give false testimony against your neighbor" (Exod. 20:16), and this commandment is repeated in Romans 13:9. In John 8:44 we are told that Satan is a liar and the father of lies, and Proverbs 6:16–17 informs us that God hates liars. Revelation 21:8, 27 and 22:15 tell us that liars will end up in hell.

We know that God can forgive any sin except the unbelief that rejects His Son, Jesus Christ. The apostle Peter didn't tell the truth when he denied the Lord, and yet he was forgiven. Believers sometimes succumb to temptation and tell a "white lie" or a "half-truth" just to stay out of trouble. Then our hearts convict us, we confess our sins, and God forgives us. God takes truth seriously, so He also takes lying seriously. Let's try to answer four questions as we consider this admonition "Do not lie to each other" (Col. 3:9).

What Is a Lie?

I suppose the simplest definition would be that a lie is a deliberate and conscious misrepresentation of the truth. A lie has to be deliberate; it isn't an unintentional mistake. If my watch isn't working properly and you ask me what time it is, I would give you the wrong time, but I am not deliberately trying to misrepresent the truth. Sometimes we fail to tell the truth by accident, and sometimes we're ignorant of the truth. But a lie is a deliberate intent to deceive.

We can lie just by saying things in a certain way. Or the inflection of our voice may make people believe that we mean something else. We can lie with our lips, and we can certainly lie with our lives as well. What we say, why we say it, and how we say it will determine whether our words are true. Philosophers debate "What is truth?" and "What is a lie?" but we'll settle for this definition: a lie is a deliberate and conscious misrepresentation of the truth.

Why Do We Lie?

It's been said that if you're going to be a liar, you had better have a good memory, because somebody will remember what you said. There's a great deal to be said for that advice! Then why do we lie? Wouldn't it be easier just to tell the truth?

Pride. Sometimes we lie because of our pride. We want to impress people with who we are or what we've done, so we exaggerate or even say what isn't true. In Acts 5 Ananias and Sapphira lied to the church and tried to lie to God because they wanted to impress people with their spirituality. Barnabas had given a gift to the church, and Ananias and Sapphira thought they would get in on some of the honor, so they lied. I don't know why we think we have to impress people. The only person we really have to please is the Lord.

Fear. Sometimes we lie because of fear. We don't want to be discovered, embarrassed, or possibly punished. We hide behind lies in order to stay out of trouble, and we end up getting into more trouble. The poet, Sir Walter Scott, has well said, "Oh, what a tangled web we weave, / When first we practice to deceive!" When we were little children, we sometimes lied, and then we had to tell another lie to cover up the first one. Before long, we were really in trouble just trying to keep track of the lies! We lie because we're afraid of what people might say or do, when we ought to tell the truth and fear God alone.

Hatred. Sometimes we lie because we want to hurt people. If we tell the truth, it might sound too good, so we make something up just to hurt them.

Unbelief. The basic reason for most lies is unbelief. We don't really believe that telling the truth is the best thing to do. But our God is the God of truth and He honors the truth. Jesus said, "I am the truth" (John 14:6), and the Holy Spirit is the Spirit of truth (16:13). God's Word is truth (17:17), and God Himself is the God of truth (Deut. 32:4). Ultimately, God blesses the truth and judges lies, but in our unbelief, we think we can get away with deception.

Sometimes telling the truth seems to get us into trouble, but if trouble does come, it's only temporary. The truth will finally prevail. When we doubt God's Word and tell a lie, we're following the devil's tactics; when we tell the truth, we walk with the Lord.

To Whom Do We Lie?

We sometimes lie to one another, and this is easy to do because other people can't read our minds or know our hearts. We lie to one another by exaggerating, by flattering people, even by the words we speak while in church. It's easy to sing "I Surrender All" while still holding on to the controls of our life. People have sung, "I'll go where you want me to go, dear Lord, . . . I'll be what you want me to be," and yet in their hearts they have no desire to do anything God wants them to do. It's possible for a soloist or a choir member to lie while singing. In one of the churches I pastored, a young lady who was out of the will of God was going to sing a solo in the morning service. I asked her, "What are you going to sing?" It was a song of dedication, and I said, "You had better not sing today, because you can't sing that song honestly." She was upset with me, but she knew I was telling the truth.

We can lie even while we're serving God. I could lie while I'm preaching. How easy it is for us preachers to give people the impression that we're very spiritual, and yet deep inside is something altogether different. We can lie in praying. How many people have stood up in a prayer meeting and said, "Lord, provide what's needed for the missionaries," and yet they haven't given one dime to missions!

We can lie to ourselves, and that's a very dangerous thing to do. First John 1:6 warns us that we're on the road to moral decay when we start lying. "If we claim to have fellowship with him yet walk in the darkness, we lie and do not live by the truth." The road downward begins right there: lying to other people and trying to make them think we're more spiritual than we really are. Verse 8 says, "If we claim to be without sin, we deceive ourselves and the truth is not in us." Now we're lying to ourselves! Some Christians who are walking in darkness actually believe they're in the light. They have sin in their lives, but they're lying to themselves and convincing themselves that it really isn't sin, and if it is sin, it isn't too bad.

Finally, in verse 10 we read: "If we claim we have not sinned, we make him out to be a liar." Now we're trying to lie to God! Of course, nobody can lie to God because God knows everything, including the things we try to hide. Ananias and Sapphira tried to lie to God and the church, but God knew their hearts. God knows the thoughts and the intents of the heart.

If we start lying to each another, before long we will be lying to ourselves, and then we'll try to lie to God. It's a dangerous path to travel!

How Should We Tell the Truth?

We don't ask *why* we should tell the truth because we know the reason: this is God's commandment. We're a part of God's new creation and have buried the old life with its deception. "Do not lie to each other, since you have taken off your old self with its practices and have put on the new self, which is being renewed in knowledge" (Col. 3:9–10). As we grow in grace, we put off the old and put on the new because we're walking in newness of life (Rom. 6:4).

We speak the truth in love. Ephesians 4:15 says we should speak the truth in love. We don't use the truth as a weapon to hurt fellow believers but as a tool to build them up. When I go to the dentist, he's usually very tender and gentle as he works on my teeth. Occasionally, when he has to do some really deep work, he gives me anesthetic to deaden the pain. I appreciate that. In the same way we are to speak the truth in love, so that even if the truth hurts, the love helps to deaden the pain.

We speak the truth with grace. Colossians 4:6 says, "Let your conversation be always full of grace, seasoned with salt, so that you may know how to answer everyone." Gracious speech comes from a heart that is filled with the grace of our Lord Jesus Christ. But along with grace there must be "salt," which in Scripture is a symbol of purity. Never say to someone, "Take this with a grain of salt." *You* put the salt in it! Be sure that your speech contains no corruption. When we speak to others, we should always speak graciously and with purity.

We speak in the name of Jesus. Colossians 3:17 says, "And whatever you do, whether in word or deed, do it all in the name of the Lord Jesus." If we can't say what we have to say in the name of Jesus Christ, then we shouldn't say it. If people know we belong to Jesus, and they catch us telling lies, what will they think of the Savior?

Never underestimate the power of words. Our tongues can be set on fire by hell (James 3:6) or by heaven (Acts 2:3–4).

"Do not lie to each other" is a needed admonition in a world that thrives on deception and in a church that has its share of hypocrisy. It would be wonderful if all of us would start being honest with God in our praying and our worship, as well as honest with each other in what we say and do. In the committee meeting, in the business meeting, in the worship service, and in private conversation, the Lord wants us to tell the truth and live the truth.

Caring Christians will not lie to each other.

14

Encourage One Another

"Therefore, encourage one another."
—1 Thessalonians 5:13

"Encourage one another daily."
—Hebrews 3:13

When I was serving in pastoral ministry, I would usually write in the front of my preaching Bible the words, "Be kind, for everyone you meet is fighting a battle." I first saw them in a book written by the British preacher John Watson (1850–1907), but I understand the statement has been around for a long time. No matter where you go, you will find people who need encouragement, and you may be just the messenger God has chosen to do the job.

The word translated "encourage" in our modern versions of the Bible is usually translated "comfort" in the Authorized Version. It comes from the Greek word *parakletos,* which means "one called alongside." "The Comforter" is one of the names of the Holy Spirit (John 14:16, 26; 15:26; 16:7) and is sometimes transliterated *Paraclete.* The Holy Spirit comes to our help and enables us when the going is tough. Our English word "comfort" comes from two Latin words that mean "with strength." When you encourage others, you help to put strength into their hearts so they won't quit. In fact, the word "courage" comes from a word that means "heart," so "encourage" means "to put heart into someone." The word "discourage" means to take away the heart and leave people with no courage at all.

We usually get discouraged when we don't feel good, when the news is bad, or when we get our eyes of faith off the Lord and start looking at the circumstances around us. That's bad enough, but when people start to paint ugly pictures of the situation, then our courage really starts to fail. I recall a member in one of the churches I pastored who was always walking in the shadows and seeing the dark side of life. From his perspective, the church couldn't really step out by faith and do anything because there was always going to be strikes at the steel mills or the oil refineries, or people were going to leave the city, or the banks were going to fail again. On the other hand, I recall faithful members who kept their eyes on the Lord, walked by faith, claimed God's promises, and encouraged us to move ahead. While pastoring that congregation, I determined to be an encourager, not a discourager, and I've tried to fulfill that commitment during more than fifty years of ministry.

Learn to Encourage Yourself

"But David found strength in the Lord his God" (1 Sam. 30:6). The Authorized Version reads, "But David encouraged himself in the Lord his God." This event took place at a time when David's life seemed to be falling apart. The enemy had invaded the city of Ziklag, where David and his men were living, and had stolen their goods, kidnapped their wives and children, and burned their houses. Besides that, David's men

104

were so grief-stricken that they were considering stoning their leader! These courageous soldiers sat on the ground and wept until they could weep no more, and David wept with them. But David did something more: he sought encouragement from the Lord.

We can't encourage others if we don't receive encouragement ourselves. Unless we've been through the furnace and experienced the encouragement that only God can give, we'll end up "miserable comforters" like Job's three friends (Job 16:2). God "comforts us in all our troubles, so that we can comfort those in any trouble with the comfort we ourselves have received from God" (2 Cor. 1:4). That's one reason why the Lord allows us to experience problems and difficulties, for then we can discover for ourselves how God encourages His own people.

David's first step was to accept the situation and deal with it realistically. Like any human being, he felt the pain and expressed his grief; but he didn't stop there. While his men were looking for somebody to blame, David was looking to the Lord. Certainly he prayed and told the Lord just how he felt, but he also asked the Lord to make him a man of faith and courage. He sought the will of the Lord and God told him what to do. David obeyed God's voice and not only rescued all the people and the goods, but he was able to defeat the enemy army and take all their loot!

"Cast all your anxiety on him because he cares for you" (1 Peter 5:7). The last half of that verse is the first step in receiving divine encouragement: realize that no matter how painful the circumstances may be or how stormy the future may look, *God cares for you*. The enemy will try to convince you that God doesn't care and that He has abandoned you, but by faith we claim God's Word. Faith means obeying God in spite of the circumstances around us, the feelings within us, or the consequences before us. Once we have rested on the Word and waited on the Lord, He can give us the directions we need to solve the problems.

The more we learn to rest in the Lord in our own trials, the better we will be able to encourage others to do so. Faith grows in the furnace, and when God allows us to go into the furnace, He keeps His eye on the clock and His hand on the thermostat. He knows how long and how much, and He never makes a mistake (see 1 Peter 4:12ff.).

There are people to whom the Lord has given a special gift of encouragement (Rom. 12:8), but all of us can learn to be better encouragers if we will let the Lord encourage us.

Learn to Listen with Your Heart

One of the great mistakes Job's friends made was that they talked more than they listened. They thought that Job would be encouraged by their explanations of God's ways and their recitations of his sins and mistakes, but his friends only made Job's situation worse. Job longed for somebody with a listening ear who would enter into "the fellowship of sharing in his sufferings" (Phil. 3:10). Yes, Job in his pain said some things about himself, his friends, and the Lord that were very wrong, but listening to unkind words is part of the ministry of encouragement. Sometimes Job was angry, but the Lord accepted his anger and waited for the right time to come to Job and tenderly deal with him.

Listening with the heart doesn't mean we agree with everything that's spoken. It simply means giving hurting people opportunities to get the poisonous emotions out of their system so they can make room for the grace of God. It does people good to share their feelings honestly, and usually while they're doing it, they start to realize how wrong they are. The listening ear joined with a listening heart detects the feelings, weighs them, and responds lovingly to them. Once the hurting person has come to that place of openness and honesty, there will be time to share the encouragement of the Lord.

Healing isn't found at the end of an argument, and "man's anger does not bring about the righteous life that God desires" (James 1:20). In order to encourage others, we must be willing to accept their feelings, not argue, and not try to force our ideas down their throats. This doesn't mean that we're passive just because we don't permit ourselves to be drawn into useless (and dangerous) theological arguments. It takes a great deal of grace and self-control to listen and not react to what we hear. "Everyone should be quick to listen, slow to speak and slow to become angry" (James 1:19). Even when the hurting person doesn't speak, we must accept the silence and empathize with it.

It isn't necessary to answer every question, correct every mistaken view, or debate every conclusion. Just listen with your heart, acknowledge the feelings being expressed, and wait for the time to come when you can share the encouragement of the Lord.

Learn to Apply the Word of God

The Bible is the Holy Spirit's chief "medicine" for healing broken hearts. When David encouraged himself in the Lord, surely he remembered the many promises God had given Israel and how He had cared for His people. During his years in the wilderness, David had learned many things about the Lord and His tender care, no doubt recalling how these lessons encouraged his heart. Perhaps he even reviewed some of his own psalms! Psalm 34 contains some wonderful words of encouragement and so do Psalms 57 and 142.

"For everything that was written in the past was written to teach us, so that through endurance and the encouragement of the Scriptures we might have hope" (Rom. 15:4). When we read the Bible, meditate on it, and trust it, the Spirit uses the Word to give us enlightenment, endurance, and encouragement. The world tells us to "Buck up!" and "Hang in there!" but those clichés don't have the power to infuse encouragement into our hearts. People are saying to us what the leader of the synagogue service said to Paul and Barnabas: "Brothers, if you have a message of encouragement for the people, please speak" (Acts 13:15). And Paul stood and gave them the Word of the Lord!

Now we better understand why the Lord puts us through trials: He wants to show us the promises and assurances in the Word that will encourage us and that we can use to encourage others. Our words may be sincere and loving, but they don't have the power to penetrate the heart as do the words of the Lord as found in Scripture. If you want to be an effective comforter, saturate yourself with the Bible and know how to bring out the verses that apply to the person you're trying to help. "Therefore encourage each other with these words" (1 Thess. 4:18). Paul reminded Timothy that the way to encourage God's people is to share the Word (2 Tim. 4:2).

In my own ministry, I've learned that the Bible passages that have comforted and encouraged me will usually do the same for those I'm trying to help. Don't be afraid to use the "golden oldies" like Psalm 23 or Romans 8, because familiar words take on new luster when you're in the furnace. The Spirit of God can help us see new truths in old verses and find new strength from familiar promises. Our prayer must always be, "Open my eyes that I may see wonderful things in your law (Ps. 119:18).

Learn to Be Faithful to the Flock

When you and I faithfully attend public worship, we are encouraging others. "Let us not give up meeting together, as some are in the habit of doing, but let us encourage one another—and all the more as you see the Day approaching" (Heb. 10:25). It's easy these days to become isolated Christians and read the Word by ourselves, pray by ourselves, and encourage ourselves, but in the end, this approach to the Christian life doesn't succeed. Whether we recognize it or not, we need each other. In fact, that saint in the local church who seems to be of least value may be the very one the Lord will use to meet a need in our life.

Many years ago, my wife and children and I were on our way to Wisconsin for a much-needed vacation. We stopped in Chicago, where I was scheduled to preach at a church pastored by a friend. During the Sunday school hour, a team from a Christian college gave a presentation and the young leader of the team spoke. I confess to my shame that I prepared myself for a shallow, immature message, but the Lord used that young man's words to encourage my heart. Our church was preparing for a building program, and I felt pushed to the limit. The message the young man brought met my needs. As I sat in the pew in tears, I asked the Lord to forgive me for being judgmental, and then I thanked Him for using that young man to minister to my heart. When I stood to preach at the service that followed, I was much better prepared.

When you go to attend public worship, ask the Lord to guide you to anybody who needs encouragement. It may be a stranger or somebody you've known for years. If we ask, "How are you?" we'll get the usual, reply, "Just fine, just fine!" But if our "spiritual radar" is working, we can detect whether or not things are really "fine." There might even be a teenager or a child, or perhaps a senior saint in a wheelchair, who just needs a smile and some strengthening words. If our question when we go to church is 'What am I going to get?" then we'll be disappointed; but if we ask, "What can I give others?" the Lord will both bless us and make us a blessing to others.

But let's not minister encouragement only on the Lord's Day when we go to church to worship. "Encourage one another daily" is the admonition of Hebrews 3:13, and by using such wonderful equipment as telephones and computers, we can reach people quickly and help them along the way. That unexpected phone call or e-mail might be just what they need to help them overcome a temptation or bear a burden.

"An anxious heart weighs a man down, but a kind word cheers him up" (Prov. 12:25). "Pleasant words are a honeycomb, sweet to the soul and healing to the bones" (Prov. 16:24).

Learn to Be a Barnabas (Acts 4:36–37)

His original name was Joseph, but he became such a great encouragement to the church in Jerusalem that the apostles gave him a nickname: Barnabas, "the son of encouragement."

To begin with, he was an encouragement in his giving. There was nothing selfish about Barnabas, for he sold his property and gave the money to the Lord. (Incidentally, his act of generosity and faith helped to expose the deception of Ananias and Sapphira.) Barnabas was also an encouragement in his friendship. When Paul came to Jerusalem, the saints were afraid of him; but Barnabas accepted him and brought him to the apostles (Acts 9:23–30). We wonder what would have happened to Paul's future ministry if Barnabas hadn't been his friend. The two men teamed up for the first missionary journey, and Barnabas proved to be a great help.

Barnabas was also a friend to his cousin John Mark (Col. 4:10), who went with Paul and Barnabas on that first missionary trip but for some reason dropped out and returned to Jerusalem (Acts 13:1–13). Later, Barnabas wanted to give Mark another chance, but Paul refused, so Barnabas took Mark with him and went in another direction (Acts 15:36–41). When it came to choosing helpers, Paul's question was, "What can he do for the work?" while Barnabas asked, "What can the work do for him?" But at the close of his ministry, Paul had to admit that Barnabas was right (2 Tim. 4:11). Barnabas was a good mentor who helped younger ministers succeed in the work of the Lord. What a blessing it would be if "retired" servants of the Lord would take time to mentor young men and women in the church, the future John Marks, who are heading for ministry.

Encouragement is one of the best expressions of Christian love, so—"Be kind, for everyone you meet is fighting a battle."

15

Stop Doing That!

The "one another" statements of Scripture that we've examined in this book have been commands that tell us how to relate positively to our fellow Christians. But there are also some negative "one another" statements in Scripture that warn us about things we should not do to one another. Living as we do in a sinful society, it's easy for us to pick up the attitudes and even the language of people in the marketplace and start to abuse God's people. In my pastoral ministry, I've seen many conflicts in families and churches caused by professed believers acting like unbelievers. We all need to take to heart these "Stop doing that!" commandments from the Lord.

Stop Biting and Devouring Each Other!

"If you keep on biting and devouring each other, watch out or you will be destroyed by each other" (Gal. 5:15). Paul sent that warning to the believers in the Galatian churches who were at war with each other. These churches had been invaded by false teachers who were telling the believers that they had to keep the law of Moses if they wanted to be good Christians. When somebody in a church starts to believe false doctrine, it always creates trouble; for if we don't believe what's right, we can't live what's right. False doctrine is like yeast that gets in secretly, spreads, and puffs up the people who accept it (Gal. 5:9). They start to act superior ("We have something you don't!") and before long, they declare war. Pride and battles usually go together.

The picture in verse 15 is that of wild animals attacking each other and refusing to give up the fight. In the end, they are all so mangled and weak that none of them really wins the battle. God's people are compared to sheep (John 10), and sheep are peaceful animals. When God's people don't "live by the Spirit" (Gal. 5:16), they live by the flesh; and the believer's sinful nature can create all sorts of problems. Among the works of the flesh are "hatred, discord, jealousy, fits of rage, selfish ambition, dissensions, factions" (v. 20). Do such things actually go on in churches? Unfortunately, they do!

Once somebody declares war in a congregation, the devil gets a foothold (Eph. 4:27) and moves in with all his artillery. I recall a congregation whose board asked an adult Sunday school class to move to a different location to make room for expansion in the children's department, but the class refused to do so. After all, the class members had purchased the rug on the floor, painted the walls, and decorated the room—and it belonged to them! The class even tried to sue the church! What a poor testimony these worldly believers were to the community.

False doctrine, pride, and selfishness work together and turn God's children into angry animals. Instead of feeding their hearts with spiritual truth, they start feeding on each other. "Let us not become conceited, provoking and envying each another" (Gal. 5:26). The believers in the Galatian churches needed a good dose of humility and love. Paul begged them to turn from false doctrine and walk in the Spirit. To live in the flesh only invites trouble and conflict.

When there's conflict among believers, people *prey on* each other instead of *praying for* each other. A retired missionary told me about a church in a field he had served that was experiencing dissension and division. People were taking sides and war was about to erupt. The elders of the church wisely announced a cessation of all public meetings and called for a time of prayer and fasting. Before long, people began to see their own sins and confess them to the Lord and to one another. God answered prayer and the Spirit brought cleansing and healing to the spiritual body.

God commands us to be at peace with one another (Mark 9:50), not to declare war on each other. When God's children disagree, they can ask the Lord to help them deal with their disagreements and speak the truth in love (Eph. 4:15). "How good and pleasant it is when brothers live together in unity!" (Ps. 133:1).

Stop Slandering One Another!

"Brothers, do not slander one another" (James 4:11). To slander people is to speak evil about them so that you damage their reputation and lower them in the esteem of others. Although it's possible to speak the truth and do it in such a way that what is said is slanderous, usually slander is manufactured by twisting the truth or telling outright lies.

Philippians 4 is the "peace chapter" of the Bible, but James 4 is the "war chapter." The believers James wrote to were involved in "fights and quarrels" (v. 1), and one of the weapons they were using was slander. Instead of being controlled by the Holy Spirit, they were living for the world (v. 4), the flesh (vv. 1, 5), and the devil (vv. 6–7). The Greek word for devil *(diabolos)* means "a slanderer"; so when we slander others, we're working in cooperation with the devil.

Moses in the law commanded the Jews not to practice slander. "Do not go about spreading slander among the people" (Lev. 19:16). It's interesting that the very next commandment (v. 17) is "Do not do anything that endangers your neighbor's life. I am the LORD." I have no more right to endanger my neighbor's reputation than I have to endanger his life. Both are destructive and both must be avoided.

Slander is often born out of a union of anger and envy. "Get rid of all bitterness, rage and anger, brawling and slander, along with every form of malice" (Eph. 4:31). When we cultivate hidden anger in our hearts, then we become bitter and envious at the success of others and we want to retaliate. One way to retaliate is to spread gossip about them. When others praise them for what they've done, we can quietly drop in some slander and poison the whole conversation.

The Jewish rabbis wrote, "The slanderous tongue kills three: the slandered, the slanderer, and him who listens to the slander." We can't sow lies about others without reaping a bitter harvest in our own lives. If every Christian obeyed 1 Corinthians 5:11, there would be many lonely people in our churches: "But now I am writing you that you must not associate with anyone who calls himself a brother but is sexually immoral or greedy, an idolater or a slanderer, a drunkard or a swindler. With such a man do not even eat." We would immediately condemn immorality and idolatry, but for some reason, we're prone to tolerate slander and even participate in it. "He who conceals his hatred has lying lips, and whoever spreads slander is a fool" (Prov. 10:18).

Stop Grumbling at Each Other!

"Don't grumble against each other, brothers, or you will be judged. The Judge is standing at the door" (James 5:9). The word translated "grumble" means "to groan inwardly but not express it." Of course, any feeling in our hearts that we try to hide will eventually come out, and it may happen at a time when we least expect it.

Grumbling at God and at God's chosen leaders was one of the chief sins of the nation of Israel in the Old Testament. No sooner had they been delivered from Egypt than they began to grumble against God and Moses because they wanted food and water. Throughout their wilderness journey, Israel frequently grumbled and God had to discipline them. "And do not grumble as some of them did—and were killed by the destroying angel" (1 Cor. 10:10). That's the negative; the positive says, "Do everything without complaining or arguing" (Phil. 2:14).

Many people today feel they are entitled to certain things, and if they don't get them, they grumble. "Entitlement" usually goes along with pride: "I deserve these things because of who I am and what I've accomplished." But we must remember that there are no seniority rights in the family of God. All true believers are one in Christ and God is no respecter of persons. No matter how many years you've been a member of the church you attend, you have no right to "pull rank" on other believers.

The hour immediately after Sunday morning worship is usually the "grumble hour" among the saints as they do an "autopsy" on the service. Since nothing we do here on earth is perfect, we can always find something to complain about. But the Lord hears our grumbling just as He heard Israel's murmuring (Exod. 16:8–9, 11), and if we don't repent, He may discipline us.

The context of this admonition is that of the farmer and his crop (James 5:7–9), and the emphasis is on patience. The farmer plows the ground, plants the seed and waters it, and then has to wait for the harvest to appear. No amount of fussing or grumbling on his part will hasten the harvest. He might grumble against some of the farmhands, but that won't accomplish anything. So it is with God's family: We must be patient with each other and with the Lord, and one day the harvest will come. We are laborers together with the Lord

117

and each other, and we should use the sickles on the harvest and not on each other.

When I served as senior pastor of a church, I usually asked other staff members to fill the pulpit if I had to be away. How else would they mature in their preaching skills if they didn't have opportunity to preach? However, some of the church members didn't like this policy and came to me with their complaints. They wanted me to invite famous preachers to the church so they could bask in their greatness. But I persisted, and I'm glad I did. Today those men are pastoring their own churches and serving God with distinction and blessing. As for the murmurers, I don't know what happened to them.

Stop Making Distinctions Among Yourselves!

"Have you not discriminated among yourselves and become judges with evil thoughts?" (James 2:4). James was here admonishing the church ushers not to cater to the wealthy and abuse the poor. The early church was comprised of free people and slaves, rich and poor, men and women, educated and uneducated, and they belonged to different races and ethnic groups. "There is neither Jew nor Greek, slave nor free, male nor female, for you are all one in Christ Jesus" (Gal. 3:28).

Much is being said these days about the various generations that the church is supposed to reach—the boomers, the busters, the builders, generation Xers, and so on. When it comes to evangelism, we need to understand how these different groups think and what approaches we should use to bring them to Christ. But once they're converted and in the church, there is no difference; and to cater to one generation at the expense of driving others away is foolish. The church is like a family and it's made up of different generations whose members love each other, care for each other, learn from each other, and help each other.

118

James is blunt: "Don't show favoritism" (2:1). He may have read Leviticus 19:15, "Do not pervert justice; do not show partiality to the poor or favoritism to the great, but judge your neighbor fairly." Paul admonished Timothy, "I charge you, in the sight of God and Christ Jesus and the elect angels, to keep these instructions without partiality, and to do nothing out of favoritism" (1 Tim. 5:21).

You and I can see only the outside of a person, but God can see the heart. A handsome or beautiful face, exquisite manners, expensive clothes, or cultured speech may impress us, but the Lord looks first at the heart. In the first century, the Jews called other peoples "barbarians" or "Gentile dogs," but in the church, Jew and Gentile are one in Christ and are both sheep. Not the color of a person's skin but the condition of a person's heart is the important thing with the Lord. When He ministered on earth, our Lord accepted all kinds of people, loved them, and saved them.

"So from now on we regard no one from a worldly point of view" (2 Cor. 5:16). Because we belong to the new creation (v. 17), we have a new Master—Jesus Christ—and we live by a new measure: seeing everyone in the light of Jesus and the cross. When I meet an unbeliever, I say, "Here is someone for whom Jesus died," and I can manifest love and kindness. Since we have a new Master and a new measure, we can fulfill our new ministry, the ministry of reconciliation (vv. 18–20). God has left us in this broken world to help put things back together, and one day He will "bring all things in heaven and on earth together under one head, even Christ" (Eph. 1:10). Christians are supposed to be peacemakers and not troublemakers.

As long as we make distinctions among ourselves, we hinder the church from being all that God wants it to be. Jesus prayed for unity, not uniformity, and unity demands diversity. When the orchestra plays in unison, we recognize the melody but we don't enjoy hearing it played that way. We want unity, the harmony produced when each instrumen-

119

talist plays his or her part and follows the same director. In the Body of Christ, there are diverse members, diverse gifts, and diverse ministries, and yet all of these work together under the lordship of Christ to accomplish God's will in this world.

The assembly to which James was writing catered to the rich and embarrassed the poor. The rich man got the best seat in the house and the poor man sat on the floor. But James reminded the believers that it was the poor whom God put first! Jesus Himself was poor and He chose to minister to the poor (2 Cor. 8:9; Luke 4:18). You can be rich in this world and poor in the next (1 Tim. 6:17–19), and you can be poor in this world and rich in the next (Matt. 5:5). It isn't a sin to be rich, for men like Abraham and David were rich, but it is a sin to put our riches ahead of God or to measure others on the basis of riches.

What's the solution to this problem of making distinctions in the church? Obeying what James calls "the royal law"— which is "Love your neighbor as yourself" (James 2:8). It's called "the royal law" not only because it came from the royal throne of God, but because it's the law that rules over every other law. If we love God and love others, we will have no problem obeying what God tells us to do (Rom. 13:8–10). Furthermore, when we obey this royal law, we live like kings! Instead of being slaves to prejudices and human measurements, we reign with Christ in the kingdom of love and enjoy spiritual freedom.

Caring Christians don't bite and devour one another. They don't slander one another or grumble at one another. They obey the royal law of love and don't make distinctions among believers based on unbiblical measurements.

They love one another, treating others the way Jesus treats them.

Can you think of a better way to live?

Warren W. Wiersbe is Distinguished Professor of Preaching at Grand Rapids Baptist Seminary and has pastored churches in Indiana, Kentucky, and Illinois (Chicago's historic Moody Church). He is the author of more than 150 books, including *God Isn't in a Hurry, The Bumps Are What You Climb On, and The Bible Exposition Commentary: New Testament* (2 vols).